The Strand I

Walter Besant and G. E. Mitton

Alpha Editions

This edition published in 2024

ISBN : 9789362997876

Design and Setting By
Alpha Editions
www.alphaedis.com
Email - info@alphaedis.com

As per information held with us this book is in Public Domain.
This book is a reproduction of an important historical work. Alpha Editions uses the best technology to reproduce historical work in the same manner it was first published to preserve its original nature. Any marks or number seen are left intentionally to preserve its true form.

Contents

PREFATORY NOTE..- 1 -

PART I WEST AND NORTH OF
CHARING CROSS..- 3 -

PART II PICCADILLY AND ST.
JAMES'S SQUARE...- 20 -

PART III THE STRAND..- 35 -

PREFATORY NOTE

A survey of London, a record of the greatest of all cities, that should preserve her history, her historical and literary associations, her mighty buildings, past and present, a book that should comprise all that Londoners love, all that they ought to know of their heritage from the past—this was the work on which Sir Walter Besant was engaged when he died.

As he himself said of it: "This work fascinates me more than anything else I've ever done. Nothing at all like it has ever been attempted before. I've been walking about London for the last thirty years, and I find something fresh in it every day."

He had seen one at least of his dreams realized in the People's Palace, but he was not destined to see this mighty work on London take form. He died when it was still incomplete. His scheme included several volumes on the history of London as a whole. These he finished up to the end of the eighteenth century, and they form a record of the great city practically unique, and exceptionally interesting, compiled by one who had the qualities both of novelist and historian, and who knew how to make the dry bones live. The volume on the eighteenth century, which Sir Walter called a "very big chapter indeed, and particularly interesting," will shortly be issued by Messrs. A. and C. Black, who had undertaken the publication of the Survey.

Sir Walter's idea was that the next two volumes should be a regular and systematic perambulation of London by different persons, so that the history of each parish should be complete in itself. This was a very original feature in the great scheme, and one in which he took the keenest interest. Enough has been done of this section to warrant its issue in the form originally intended, but in the meantime it is proposed to select some of the most interesting of the districts and publish them as a series of booklets, attractive alike to the local inhabitant and the student of London, because much of the interest and the history of London lie in these street associations. For this purpose Chelsea, Westminster, the Strand, and Hampstead have been selected for publication first, and have been revised and brought up to date.

The difficulty of finding a general title for the series was very great, for the title desired was one that would express concisely the undying charm of London—that is to say, the continuity of her past history with the present times. In streets and stones, in names and palaces, her history is written for those who can read it, and the object of the series is to bring forward these associations, and to make them plain. The solution of the difficulty was found in the words of the man who loved London and planned the great scheme. The work "fascinated" him, and it was because of these associations that it did so. These links between past and present in themselves largely constitute The Fascination of London.

G. E. M.

PART I
WEST AND NORTH OF CHARING CROSS

Beginning at the extreme westerly limit of St. Martin's-in-the-Fields, on the south side of Hyde Park Corner, we find ourselves in the Green Park. This is a triangular piece of ground, which was formerly called Little or Upper St. James's Park. It has not much history. In 1642 fortifications were erected on Constitution Hill, and at the end of the seventeenth century this same spot was a noted place for duels. Fireworks on a great scale, with public entertainments, took place in the park at the Peace of Aix-la-Chapelle, and again in 1814. On Constitution Hill three attempts were made on the life of Queen Victoria. The chief object of interest in the park is Buckingham Palace, which is not altogether in St. Martin's; in fact, the greater part, including most of the grounds, is in the adjacent parish of St. George's, Hanover Square. The palace is a dreary building, without any pretence of architectural merit, but it attracts attention as the London home of the English Sovereign.

It stands on the site of Arlington House, so called from its connection with Henry Bennet, Earl of Arlington (the Earl whose initial supplied one of the *a's* in the word "Cabal"). John Sheffield, Duke of Buckingham, bought the house and rebuilt it in 1703, naming it after himself, and including in the grounds part of the land belonging to Tart Hall, which stood at the head of St. James's Street, and has been mentioned in the account of the adjoining parish of St. Margaret's, Westminster. Buckingham House was bought from Sir Charles Sheffield, son of the above-mentioned Duke, by the Crown in 1762. In 1775 it was granted to Queen Charlotte as a place of residence in lieu of Somerset House, and at this period it was known as Queen's House. George IV. employed Nash to renovate the building, and the restoration was so complete as to amount to an entire rebuilding, in the style considered then fashionable; the result is the present dreary building with stuccoed frontage. The interior is handsome enough, and, like that of many a London house of less importance, is considerably more cheerful than the exterior. The chief staircase is of white marble, and the rooms are richly decorated. The state apartments include drawing-rooms, saloons, and the throne-room, which is sixty-four feet in length. The picture-gallery contains a collection of pictures made by George IV., chiefly of the Dutch school; it includes works of Rembrandt, Rubens, Vandyck, Dürer, Cuyp, Ruysdael, Vandervelde, and others.

The grounds are about forty acres in extent, and contain a large piece of ornamental water, on the shore of which is a pavilion, or summer-house, with frescoes by Eastlake, Maclise, Landseer, Dyce, and others, illustrating Milton's "Comus." The channel of the Tyburn, now a sewer, passes under the palace. The Marble Arch, at the north-east corner of Hyde Park, was first designed to face the palace, where it stood until 1850.

The palace is partly on the site of the well-known Mulberry Gardens, a place of entertainment in the seventeenth century. These gardens originated in an order of James I., who wished to encourage the rearing of silkworms in England. This project, like many others of the same King, proved a failure, and the gardens were turned into a place of public recreation. The frequenters were of the fashionable classes, and came in the evening to sit in small arbours, and "be regaled with cheesecakes, syllabubs, and wine sweetened with sugar." In this form the place was extremely popular, and is often mentioned in contemporary literature. Dryden came there to eat tarts with "Mrs." Anne Reeve, and doubtless Evelyn and Pepys often strolled about in the gay crowd, a crowd much gayer than it would now be—in the matter of costume, at all events. The scene of "The Mulberry Gardens," a play by Sir Charles Sedley (1668) is laid here.

Stafford House, not far from St. James's Palace, and overlooking the Green Park, is now tenanted by the Duke of Sutherland. It was originally built for the Duke of York, brother to George IV., but he died before its completion. It stands on the site of an older building, called Godolphin House, and also occupies the site of the Queen's Library formed by Caroline, wife of George IV.

St. James's Palace is divided into many sets of apartments and suites of rooms, and in this way resembles more the ancient than the modern idea of a palace. On its site once stood a hospital for fourteen leprous women, which was founded, as Stow quaintly says, "long before the time of any man's memory." Maitland says the hospital must have been standing before 1100 A.D., as it was then visited by the Abbot of Westminster. Eight brethren were subsequently added to the institution. Several benevolent bequests of land were made to it from time to time. In 1450 the custody of the hospital was granted perpetually to Eton College by Henry VI. In 1531 Henry VIII. obtained some of the neighbouring land from the Abbey of Westminster, and in the following year he took the hospital also, giving lands in Suffolk in exchange for it. There is reason to believe that he pensioned off the ejected inmates. At any rate, having demolished the House of Mercy, he proceeded to build for himself a palace, which is supposed to have been planned by Holbein, under the direction of Cromwell, Earl of Essex. Henry VIII. was too much occupied in taking possession of Wolsey's palaces to bestow very much of his time on his own new building, though he occasionally resided here before he acquired Whitehall. Edward VI. did not live at St James's Palace regularly, but Queen

Mary patronized it, preferring it to Whitehall. It was granted to Prince Henry during the reign of James I., and Charles I. spent the last three days before his execution here. The Prince known as the "Pretender" was born in one of the palace apartments, and many historians have commented on the fact that this chamber was conveniently near a small back-staircase, up which a new-born infant could have been smuggled. During the reign of King William the palace was fitted up as a residence for Prince George of Denmark and Princess Anne. When the Princess ascended the throne, the palace became the regular residence of the Court, which it continued to be until the accession of Queen Victoria, who preferred Buckingham Palace.

The only parts remaining of King Henry's building are the gatehouse, some turrets, a mantelpiece in the presence chamber, which bears the initials H. and A. (Henry and Anne Boleyn) with a true lovers' knot, the Chapel Royal (which has, of course, been renovated), and the tapestry-room. Levées are still held at the palace.

On the west of the gatehouse a series of apartments were being prepared for the Duke of Clarence at the time of his death, and were afterwards assigned to the present Prince and Princess of Wales. At the west end is Clarence House, in the occupation of the Duke of Connaught. This was occupied by the King of Prussia and his sons on their visit to England in 1814. The Duchess of Kent resided here until 1861.

The Lord Chamberlain's offices and residence, and also the official residence of the Keeper of the Privy Purse, are among the official chambers in the palace. There are minor offices also, those of the Clerk of the Works, and the Gentlemen of the Wine Cellar; there are state apartments and the quarters of the Gentlemen at Arms and the Yeomen of the Guard. There are several courts in the palace, namely, the Ambassadors' Court, Engine Court, Friary Court, and Colour Court. There have been various chapels connected with the palace, but the only two of importance are the Chapel Royal and German Chapel, which still remain.

The Chapel Royal is supposed to be on the site of the chapel of the ancient hospital, and various Norman remains dug up in the course of repairs favour this supposition. The roof is beautifully decorated in panels by Holbein; the date of its completion is supposed to be 1540. Prince George and Princess Anne; Frederick, Prince of Wales; George IV.; Queen Victoria; and the Empress Frederick, were all married in this Chapel.

The German Chapel was founded in 1700 by Princess Anne; service was held in it once on Sundays up to the present reign, but has now been discontinued.

Just opposite to the palace is Marlborough House, the residence of the Prince and Princess of Wales. The house was built in 1709 at the public expense, as a national compliment to the Duke of Marlborough. Sir Christopher Wren was the architect. After the death of the third Duke it was sublet to Leopold, subsequently King of the Belgians. Queen Adelaide lived in it after the death of King William IV. The building was afterwards used as a gallery for the pictures known as the Vernon Collection. But in 1850 it was settled on King Edward VII., then Prince of Wales, when he should attain his eighteenth year, which he did nine years later. The interior is decorated with beautiful mural paintings executed by La Guerre; many of these represent the battles of the famous Duke of Marlborough. On the removal of the King to Buckingham Palace the present Prince of Wales comes in his turn to Marlborough House.

Carlton House Terrace owes its name to Carlton House, built by Henry Boyle, Baron Carlton, in Queen Anne's reign. It was afterwards sold to Frederick, Prince of Wales, and was occupied subsequently by George IV. before he succeeded to the throne. J. T. Smith says: "Many a saturnalia did those walls witness in the days of his hot youth." Princess Charlotte was born here. In 1811 the ceremony of conferring the regency upon Prince George was enacted at Carlton House, and in the June following the Prince gave a magnificent supper to 2,000 guests. In 1827 the house was pulled down. It stood right across the end of the present Waterloo Place, where now a flight of steps lead into the park. At the head of the steps is the York Column of granite, 124 feet high, designed by Wyatt, and surmounted by a figure of the Duke of York, son of George III.

One of the sights of London in the seventeenth century, was the garden which lay between St. James's Park and Charing Cross, called Spring Gardens. The place was laid out as a bowling-green; it had also butts, a bathing-pond, a spring made to scatter water all around by turning a wheel. There was also an ordinary, which charged 6s. for a dinner—then an enormous price—and a tavern where drinking of wine was carried on all day long. In the "Character of England," 1659, attributed to Evelyn, the following account of Spring Gardens is found:

"The manner is as the company returned [from Hyde Park] to alight at the Spring Gardens so called, in order to the Parke, as our Thuilleries is to the Course; the inclosure not disagreeable, for the solemness of the grove is broken by the warbling of the birds, as it opens into the spacious walks at St. James's; but the company walk in it at such a rate, you would think that all the ladies were so many Atalantas contending with their wooers.... But fast as they run they stay there so long as if they wanted not time to finish the race; for it is usual here to find some of the young company till midnight; and the thickets of the garden seem to be contrived to all advantages of gallantry; after they have been refreshed with the collation, which is here seldom omitted, at a certain cabaret, in the middle of this paradise, where the forbidden fruits are certain trifling tarts, neats' tongues, salacious meats, and bad Rhenish; for which the gallants pay sauce, as indeed they do at all such houses throughout England."

After the Restoration the gardens were built over. Prince Rupert lived here 1674-1682. Colley Cibber, actor and prolific dramatist, had a house "near Bull's Head Tavern in Spring Gardens, 1711-14"; Sir Philip Warwick and George Canning were also among the residents.

"Locket's ordinary, a house of entertainment much frequented by gentry," was on the site of Drummond's Bank:

"Come, at a crown ahead ourselves we'll treat:Champagne our liquor, and ragouts our meat;   *   *   *   *   * With evening wheels we'll drive about the Park,Finish at Locket's, and reel home i' the dark."

Vague rumour assigns an earlier house to Cromwell on the same spot. The bank was established about 1712 by Mr. Andrew Drummond, a goldsmith. George III. transferred his account from Coutts' to Drummond's when he was displeased with the former firm, and he desired Messrs. Drummond to make no advances to Frederick, Prince of Wales, who also had an account here. This order was obeyed, with the consequences that in the succeeding reign the royal account was transferred again to Messrs. Coutts. The County Council offices are at present a very noticeable feature in Spring Gardens, and the aspect of the place is no longer rural.

The part of Whitehall included in St. Martin's parish is not very large, yet it is of some importance. On the west side is Old Scotland Yard, for long associated with the headquarters of the Metropolitan Police, now removed to New Scotland Yard. Stow says:

"On the left hand from Charing Cross are also divers tenements lately built till ye come to a large plot of ground inclosed with brick, and is called Scotland, where great buildings have been for receipt of the Kings of Scotland and other estates of that country, for Margaret Queen of Scots and sister to King Henry VIII. had her abiding here when she came to England after the death of her husband, as the Kings of Scotland had in former times when they came to the Parliament of England."

Here for some time was the official residence of the Surveyor of Works to the Crown, and Inigo Jones and Sir Christopher Wren were both occupants. Sir J. Vanbrugh also resided at Scotland Yard, and as Secretary to the Council Milton had an official residence here before he went to Petty France, as described in the book on Westminster in the same series.

Craig's or Cragg's Court, in which is the Royal Almonry office, is shown in old maps. Strype speaks of it as a "very handsome large Court, with new buildings fit for gentry of Repute." It was built in 1702, and is supposed to have been called after the father of Secretary Craggs, who was a friend of Pope and Addison. Woodfall, the publisher, had a West End office in the court, and Romney the painter lived there. There is a fine old Queen Anne house still standing at the back of the court.

Opposite Scotland Yard is the Admiralty, built round a courtyard, and hidden by a stone screen surmounted by sea-horses. The screen was the work of the brothers Adam, and was put up to hide a building which even the taste of George III.'s reign declared to be insufferable. This had been built for the Admiralty in 1726, and replaced old Wallingford House, so called from its first owner, Viscount Wallingford, who built it in the reign of James I. George Villiers, the well-known Duke of Buckingham, bought the house, and used it until his death. Archbishop Usher saw the execution of Charles I. from the roof, and swooned with horror at the sight. The house was occupied by Cromwell's son-in-law, General Fleetwood, and in 1680 became Government property. In one of the large rooms the body of Nelson lay in state before his national funeral.

St. Catherine's Hermitage, Charing Cross, stood somewhere near Charing Cross. It is believed to have been about the position of the post-office. It belonged to the See of Llandaff, and was occasionally used as a lodging by such Bishops of that See as came to attend the Court and had no town-house.

St. Mary Rounceval, on the site of Northumberland House, was founded by William Marischal, Earl of Pembroke, in Henry III.'s reign. The Earl gave several tenements to the Prior of Rounceval, in Navarre, who established here the chief house of the priory in England. The hospital was finally suppressed by Edward VI. The little village of Charing then stood between London and Westminster. It formed part of the great demesne belonging to the Abbey of Westminster, and was inhabited chiefly by Thames fishermen, who had a settlement on the bank, and by the farmers of the Westminster estates. The derivation of the name from *La Chère Reine* is purely fanciful.

There is certainly no part of London which has been so much changed as Charing Cross. In other parts the houses are changed, but the streets remain. Here the whole disposition of the streets has been transformed. The secondary part of the name recalls the beautiful cross, the last of the nine which marked the places where Queen Eleanor's coffin rested on its journey from Lincolnshire to Westminster Abbey. The cross was destroyed by the fanatical zeal of the Reformers. The equestrian statue of Charles I., cast in 1633 by Le Sœur, occupies the site of the cross. It had not been set up when the Civil War broke out, and was sold by the Parliament to John Rivit, a brazier, who lived by the Holborn Conduit, on condition that it should be broken up. John Rivit, however, buried the statue, and dug it up again after the Restoration. It was not until 1674 that it was actually erected, on a new pedestal made by Grinling Gibbons, in the place which it now occupies, which is the site of the old cross, the place where the regicides were executed, and where the Charing Cross pillory stood. It is curious to remark on the preservation of the site of the cross. It was apparently railed in; some of the stones of which it was made were used in paving Whitehall. Ballads were written on its destruction:

"Undone, undone, the lawyers are;
They wander about the towne,
Nor can find the way to Westminster
Now Charing Cross is downe.
At the end of the Strand they make a stand,
Swearing they are at a loss,
And chaffing say that's not the way,
They must go by Charing Cross."

CUNNINGHAM.

Many of the regicides were executed at this spot in Charles II.'s reign, within sight of the place where they had murdered their King. These men, according to the brutal temper of the times, were cut down when half hanged and disembowelled before a great concourse of people. Pepys mentions going to the executions as to a show. Later the pillory stood here in which, among others, Titus Oates suffered. But, besides these dismal reminiscences, Charing Cross was at one time famed for its taverns and festive places of amusement, and was the resort of wits and literati in the eighteenth century. Dr. Johnson speaks of the "full tide of human existence" being at Charing Cross, and if he could see it now he might be confirmed in his opinion.

At the top of the present Northumberland Avenue stood formerly Northumberland House, the last of the Strand palaces to be destroyed, and until its destruction the chief glory and ornament of the street and Charing Cross. It was never an episcopal palace, having been built in 1605 by the Earl of Northampton; from him it went to the Earl of Suffolk, and was called for a time Suffolk House; in 1642 it fell into the hands of the Earl of Northumberland, and by marriage into those of the Duke of Somerset until 1749, when the daughter of the Duke of Somerset succeeded, and by her marriage with Sir Hugh Smithson the house became the property of this family, now Dukes of Northumberland, until its compulsory sale in the year 1874. The house originally consisted of three sides of a quadrangle, the fourth side lying open with gardens stretching down to the river. The front was wrongly attributed to Inigo Jones. The house had been repaired or rebuilt in many places, so that there was not much that was ancient left in its later days. By the side of Northumberland House formerly ran Hartshorn Lane, now entirely obliterated. Ben Jonson was born here, and lived here in his childhood.

Trafalgar Square was built over the site of what was formerly the Royal Mews, a building of very ancient foundation; and a rookery of obscure and ill-famed lanes and alleys on the west and north of St. Martin's Church, popularly known as the Bermudas, and afterwards the Caribbean Islands. In the midst of the mews stood a small and remarkable building called Queen Elizabeth's Bath. It is almost impossible to estimate the difference between the then and the now, in regard to this particular part. St. Martin's Lane continued right up to Northumberland House, where the lion of the proud Percies stiffened his tail on the parapet. The house stood across the present head of Northumberland Avenue. The Royal Mews themselves were where the fountains now splash, and on the further side of them was Hedge Lane.

Pennant says the Mews was so called from having been used for the King's falcons—at least, from the time of Richard III. to Henry VIII. In the latter King's reign the royal horses were stabled here, but the name Mews was retained, and has come to be applied to any town range of stabling. The mews were removed to make way for the National Gallery about 1834. Geoffrey Chaucer, the poet, was Clerk of the King's Works, and of the Mews at Charing about the end of Richard II.'s reign. During the Commonwealth Colonel Joyce was imprisoned in the Mews by order of Oliver Cromwell.

It is supposed that we are indebted to William IV. for the idea of a square to be called Trafalgar in honour of Nelson, and to contain some worthy memorial of the hero. The total height of the monument, designed by Railton, is 193 feet, and its design is from that of one of the columns of the Temple of Mars at Rome. The statue, which looks so small from the ground, is really 17 feet high, nearly three times the height of a man; it was the work of E. H. Baily, R.A. The pedestal has bronze bas-reliefs on its four sides, representing the four greatest of Nelson's battles, Trafalgar, St. Vincent, Aboukir, and Copenhagen. The massive lions on the extended pedestal were designed by Sir Edwin Landseer.

Of the other statues, that of George IV. is by Sir Francis Chantrey, and was originally intended for the top of the Marble Arch, and that of General Gordon was designed by Hamo Thorneycroft. Bronze blocks let into the north wall of the square contain the measures of the secondary standards of length, and were inserted here in 1876 by the Standards Department of the Board of Trade. The Union Club and College of Physicians are on the west side of the square. The latter was founded by Dr. Linacre, physician to King Henry VIII.

The National Gallery was not designed as it now stands, but grew gradually. The idea of a collection of national pictures began in 1824, when the Angerstein Collection of thirty-eight pictures was purchased. The building began in 1832, and was opened six years later, but there were then only six rooms devoted to the national collection, the remainder being used by the Royal Academy of Arts. The Academy, however, betook itself to Burlington House in 1869, and subsequently the National Gallery was enlarged, and is now well worthy of its name. The English are taunted with not being an artistic nation; this may be, but they recognise merit when they see it, and the national collection need fear comparison with no other in the world. The sections of the gallery include Italian schools, schools of the Netherlands and Germany, Spanish, French, and British schools; in the last named the Turner Collection claims two rooms.

St. Martin's Church was founded by Henry VIII., who disliked to see the funerals of the inhabitants passing through Whitehall on their way to St. Margaret's, Westminster, but there had probably been an ecclesiastical building on or near this site from a very early date. In 1222 there was a controversy between the Bishop of London and the Dean and Chapter of St. Paul's on the one hand and the Abbot and Canons of Westminster on the other, as to the exemption of the chapel and convent of the latter from the jurisdiction of the former. The matter was settled in favour of Westminster. It is probable that this chapel was for the use of the monks when they visited their convent garden.

In 1721 the old church was pulled down, and a new one built from the designs of Gibbs the architect, whose bust stands in the building near the entrance. A rate was levied on the parish for expenses, but money poured in so liberally that a gift of £500 toward the enrichment of the altar was declined.

The building has been derided, but it has the merit of a bold conception. Ralph in "Publick Buildings" says: "The portico is at once elegant and august, and the steeple above it ought to be considered one of the most tolerable in town. The east end is remarkably elegant, and very justly challenges a particular applause; in short, if there is anything wanting in this fabric, it is a little more elevation."

The only original features in the interior are the two royal pews, not now used, which look down on the altar. St. Martin's is the royal parish, including in its boundaries Buckingham Palace and St. James's, but the births of the Royal Family are not registered here, as has been frequently stated. There is no monument in the church of any intrinsic interest, and the only other noticeable details are two beautiful mosaic panels on either side of the chancel, put up by Lady Frederick Cavendish to the memory of her husband.

Among the names of those buried in the old church is that of Vansomer, a portrait-painter. Nell Gwynne, Roubiliac, and Jack Sheppard—whose first theft took place at Rummer's Tavern, near Charing Cross—lie in the burial-ground. There is a large crypt, with vaulted roof, below the church, and here are several monuments from the old building, and also the ancient whipping-post.

Before the erection of the palaces along the riverside the fishermen of the Thames lived beside the river bank at Charing Cross. A piece of ground in the churchyard of St. Martin's was set apart for their use and kept separate. Meantime, as one after the other of the Bishops' town-houses were built, the fishermen found themselves pushed farther up the river, until finally they were fairly driven away, and established themselves at Lambeth, where the last of them lived in the early part of the nineteenth century. Their burial-ground, meantime, was preserved even after they had disappeared. The churchyard of St. Martin's was curtailed in 1826, and the parish burial-ground removed to Pratt Street, Camden Town.

Behind the National Gallery is the National Portrait Gallery, opened in 1896, and opposite to it St. Martin's Town Hall, with the parish emblem— St. Martin dividing his cloak with a beggar—in bas-relief on the frontage.

Charing Cross Road is very modern. It was opened in 1887, and swept over a number of narrow courts and alleys.

For St. Martin's Lane, see p. 16.

In this is the Public Library, where some watercolours and old prints of vanished houses are hung on the staircase. There is also the eighteenth-century plan from Strype's Survey, well worth studying.

Leicester Square, at first known as Leicester Fields, is associated with the Sidneys, Earls of Leicester, who had a town-house on the north side, where the Empire Music-hall is now. This was a large brick building, with a courtyard before it and a Dutch garden at the back. During the reign of Charles I. and in the time of the Commonwealth the Sidneys tenanted it, but later it was occupied by foreign Ambassadors. Elizabeth, Queen of Bohemia, took it in 1662, and afterwards it was aptly described by Pennant as "the pouting-place of Princes"; for George, son of George I., established here a rival Court when he had quarrelled with his father, and his son

Frederick, the Prince of Wales, did precisely the same thing. During the latter tenancy a large building adjoining, called Savile or Ailesbury House, was amalgamated with Leicester House. George III. was living here when hailed King. Savile House stood until the Gordon Riots, when it was completely stripped and gutted by the rioters. The square was presented to the public in 1874 by Baron Albert Grant, M.P. The gift is recorded on the pedestal of the statue of Shakespeare standing in the centre.

The square was for long a favourite place for duels. A line drawn diagonally from the north-east to the south-west corner roughly indicates the boundary of St Martin's parish, the upper half of the square being in St. Anne's, Soho.

The associations of this part are numerous and very interesting. The busts of the four men standing in the corners of the centre garden have all some local connection. They are those of Hogarth, Sir Joshua Reynolds, Sir Isaac Newton, and John Hunter. Hogarth's house was on the east, on the site of Tenison's School, and next to it was that of John Hunter, the famous surgeon. Sir Joshua Reynolds bought No. 47 on the west side in 1760, and lived in it until his death. Sir Isaac Newton lived in the little street off the south side of the square, at the back of the big new Dental Hospital. His house is still standing, and bears a tablet of the Society of Arts. It is quite unpretentious—a stucco-covered building with little dormer-windows in the roof. The great scientist came here in 1710, when he was nearly sixty, and his fame was then world-wide. Men from all parts of Europe sought the dull little street in order to converse with one whose power had wrought a revolution in the methods of scientific thought. In the same house Miss Burney afterwards lived with her father. Sir Thomas Lawrence took apartments at No. 4, Leicester Square, in 1786, when only seventeen, but he had already begun to exhibit at the Royal Academy. The square was for long a favourite place of residence with foreigners, and has not even yet lost a slightly un-English aspect.

Archbishop Tenison's School is at the south-east corner of the square. Its founder, who was successively Bishop of Lincoln and Archbishop of Canterbury, intended that it should counterbalance a flourishing Roman Catholic school in the Savoy precincts. Among old boys may be mentioned Postlethwaite, afterwards Master of St. Paul's; Charles Mathews, when very young; Horne Tooke a former Lord Mayor of London; and Liston who was for a time usher.

As stated above, the northern half of the square is in the parish of St. Anne's, Soho, a parish now tenanted to a very large extent by foreigners, chiefly French and Italians. Shaftesbury Avenue, running diagonally through the parish, is of very recent origin.

Soho has been derived from the watchword of Monmouth at Sedgemoor, because the Duke had a house in Soho, then King's Square. It is much more likely that the reverse is the case, and the Duke took the watchword from the locality in which he lived, for the word Soho occurs in the rate-books long before the Battle of Sedgemoor was fought. In 1634 So-howe appears in State papers; and various other spellings are extant, as Soe-hoe, So-hoe. This district was at one time a favourite hunting-ground, and Halliwell-Phillipps in the "Dictionary of Archaic and Provincial Words" suggests that the name has arisen from a favourite hunting cry, "So-ho!"

The parish was first made independent of St. Martin's in 1678. Soho has always been a favourite locality with foreigners. There were three distinct waves of emigration which flooded over it: first after the revocation of the Edict of Nantes in 1635; then in 1798, during the Reign of Terror; and thirdly in 1871, when many Communists who had escaped from Paris found their way to England. At the present time half the population of the parish consists of foreigners, of which French and Italians preponderate, but Swiss, Germans, and specimens of various other nationalities, are frequently to be met with in the streets.

The parish church of St. Anne's was so named "after the mother of the Virgin Mary and in compliment to Princess Anne." The site was a piece of ground known as Kemp's Field, and the architect selected was Sir Christopher Wren. The building is in all respects like others of its period, but has a curious spire added later. This has been described as "two hogsheads placed crosswise, in the ends of which are the dials of the clock," and above is a kind of pyramid, ending in a vane.

The old churchyard lies above the level of the street, and has been turned into a public garden. Facing the principal entrance in Wardour Street is a stone monument to King Theodore of Corsica, and a small crown on the stone marks his rank. King Theodore died in this parish December 11, 1756, immediately after leaving the King's Bench Prison, by the benefit of the Act of Insolvency, in consequence of which he registered his kingdom of Corsica for the use of his creditors.

His epitaph was written by Horace Walpole:

"The grave, great teacher, to a level brings
Heroes and beggars, galley slaves and kings.
But Theodore this moral learned ere dead:
Fate poured its lessons on his living head,
Bestowed a kingdom, but denied him bread."

Close by is a monument to the essayist Hazlitt, born 1778, died 1830. The inscription says that he lived to see his deepest wishes gratified as he expressed them in his essay on the "Fear of Death," and proceeds to set forth at considerable length the tenor of those wishes.

During the dinner-hour, when the weather is fine, the graveyard seats are filled by the very poorest of the poor, many of them aliens, far from their own country, and sad beneath the gray skies of the land that gives them bread, but denies them sun.

In the registers are recorded the baptisms of two of the children of George II., and five of the children of Frederick, Prince of Wales, born at Leicester House, in this parish.

Wardour Street has long been celebrated for its shops of old china, bric-à-brac, and furniture. It can claim Flaxman among its bygone residents.

Dean Street is a long and narrow thoroughfare, a favourite residence with artists at the end of the eighteenth century; the names of Hayman, Baily, Ward, and Belines are all to be found here in association. Sir James Thornhill lived at No. 75, where there are the remains of some curious staircase paintings by him, in the composition of which he is said to have been assisted by his son-in-law, Hogarth. Turner, the father of the great painter, was a hairdresser in Dean Street, and Nollekens' father died in No. 28. In the house adjoining the Royalty Theatre Madame Vestris was born.

Frith Street in old maps is marked "Thrift Street," a name by no means inappropriate at the present time. It also has its associations, and can claim the birth of Sir Samuel Romilly, the great law reformer, who lived until the early part of the nineteenth century, and whose father was a jeweller here; the early boyhood of Mozart, and the death of Hazlitt, which took place in furnished lodgings. The failure of his publishers had made him short of money; he was harassed by pecuniary cares, yet his last words were: "I've had a happy life."

The following advertisement bearing date March 8, 1765, is worth quotation: "Mr. Mozart, the father of the celebrated Young Musical Family who have so justly raised the Admiration of the greatest musicians of Europe, proposes to give the Public an opportunity of hearing these young Prodigies perform both in public and private, by giving on the 13th of this month a concert which will be chiefly conducted by his Son, a boy of eight years of age, with all the overtures of his own composition. Tickets may be had at 5s. each at Mr. Mozart's, or at Mr. Williamson's in Thrift Street, Soho, where Ladies and Gentlemen will find the Family at Home every day in the week from 12 to 2 o'clock and have an opportunity of putting his talents to a more particular proof by giving him anything to play at sight or any Music without a Bass, which he will write upon the spot without recurring to his harpsichord."

In this street there are many interesting relics of bygone splendour. No. 9—now to let—has a splendid well staircase with spiral balusters. The walls and ceiling of this are lined with oil-paintings of figures larger than life. These have unfortunately been somewhat knocked about during successive tenancies, but clearly show that the house was one of considerable importance in past times. It was in lodgings in this street that Mrs. Inchbald wrote her "Simple Story," published 1791, in four volumes, which was an immediate success. She was an actress as well as an author, and a friend of the Kembles. Her dramatic writings were very many.

At No. 13, Greek Street were Wedgwood's exhibition-rooms. In No. 27 De Quincey used to sleep on the floor by permission of Brumel, the money-lender's attorney.

On the other side of Shaftesbury Avenue, and parallel with it, is Gerrard Street, a dingy, unpretending place, but thick with memories and associations. It was built about 1681, and was called after Gerard, Earl of Macclesfield. Wheatley quotes from the Bagford MSS. of the British Museum to the effect that "Henry, Prince of Wales, son of James I., caused a piece of ground near Leicester Fields to be walled in for the exercise of arms. Here he built a house, which was standing at the Restoration. It afterwards fell into the hands of Lord Gerard, who let the ground out to build upon." Hatton speaks of "Macclesfield House, alias Gerrard House, a well-built structure situate in Gerrard Street ... now (1708) in possession of Lord Mohun." Dryden lived in Gerrard Street in a house on the site of one marked by a tablet of the Society of Arts. He died here, and his funeral was interrupted by a drunken frolic of Mohocks headed by Lord Jeffreys. Close by is an hotel, where once Edmund Burke resided; opposite to him J. T. Smith lodged, as he tells us in "Nollekens and his Times," and he could look into Burke's rooms when they were lighted, and see the patient student at work until the small hours of the morning. Charles Kemble and his family also resided in this street.

On the site of the Westminster General Dispensary was a tavern named the Turk's Head, where the well-known literary club had its origin. The members were at first twelve in number, including Sir Joshua Reynolds, Dr. Johnson, Edmund Burke, Dr. Nugent, Topham Beauclerk, Mr. Langton, Dr. Goldsmith, and Sir J. Hawkins. In 1772 the number of the members was increased to twenty, and instead of meeting weekly, on Mondays, for a supper, they met every fortnight, on a Friday, and dined together. David Hume was here in 1758, and the actor Edmund Kean passed most of his boyhood in this street, sheltered by a couple who had adopted him when his mother deserted him in Frith Street. All his early boyhood is associated with this neighbourhood; he was found in Frith Street, and his schools were in Orange Court, Leicester Square, and Chapel Street, Soho. The dispensary is in itself interesting, being one of the very oldest institutions of the kind, established in 1774.

Charing Cross Road follows very nearly the course of the old Hog Lane, later Crown Street, which bounded the parish on the east. St. Mary the Virgin's Church is on the west side, and the building has had many vicissitudes. In 1677 it was erected by the Greek congregation in Soho, and had the distinction of being the first church of that community in England. It was afterwards used by a French Protestant community, and then by a body of Dissenters. In 1849 it stood in imminent peril of being turned into a dancing-saloon, but was rescued and became Church of England.

The very centre and nucleus of the parish has always been Soho Square, which was built in the reign of Charles II., and was at first called King Square—not in compliment to the monarch, but after a man named Gregory King, who was associated with the earliest buildings. It is a place of singular attractiveness, an oasis in a desert; many of the houses are picturesque. The square garden is not large, but it is planted with fine trees. From the very beginning the square was an aristocratic locality, and the houses tenanted by the nobility; the most important of these, Monmouth House, occupied the whole of the southern side. This was architecturally a very extraordinary building, and the interior was very magnificent. "The principal room on the ground-floor was a dining-room, the carved and gilt panels of which contained whole-length pictures. The principal room on the first-floor was lined with blue satin superbly decorated with pheasants and other birds in gold. The chimneypiece was richly ornamented with fruit and foliage; in the centre, within a wreath of dark leaves, was a circular recess for a bust" ("Nollekens and his Times").

The Duke of Monmouth obtained the site for this house in 1681, but he did not long enjoy his possession, for four years later he suffered the penalty of his pretensions and was executed. The house was later occupied by successive French Ambassadors; it was demolished in 1773. The houses at present standing at the south end of the square must have been built immediately after the destruction of Monmouth House, and possibly the materials of the older building were used in their construction. The Hospital for Women shows some traces of former grandeur in panelled rooms and decorative cornices. The hospital was only established in these quarters in 1851, so the house may have had fashionable tenants before.

On the same side is the Rectory House, which was probably built directly after the demolition of Monmouth House in 1773. Here there are to be found all the characteristics of an eighteenth-century building, including a decorative ceiling by Flaxman. In the south-west corner of the square there is the house in which is now the Hospital for Diseases of the Heart and Paralysis. This was at one time the headquarters of the Linnæan Society, before its removal to Burlington House. It contains some beautiful ceilings and cornices, and one room, now a female ward, is worthy of special notice. A very lofty arched ceiling of rather unusual construction is beautifully decorated, and the overmantel and fireplace are exquisite.

In the opposite or south-east corner of the square is the House of Charity. This was formerly the residence of Alderman Beckford, twice Lord Mayor of London in George III.'s reign, who was credited with being the only man of his day who dared tell the King the truth to his face. His son was the author of "Vathek." The house is now a house of mercy, for the assistance of orphans, homeless girls, and all who, through no fault of their own, find themselves without a roof to shelter them or work to do. The charity is Church of England, and under the direction of a Warden and Council. The fine decorative wooden overmantels and doorways still remain, and the joints and edges of the panels are all carved, which gives a very handsome appearance to some of the rooms. The council-room ceiling is a large oval with the figures of four cherubic boys in relief, carrying respectively flowers, a bird, fire, and water, to represent the four elements.

One of the former famous houses in the square was Carlisle House. The walls were of red brick, and the date on the cisterns 1669, the date of the creation of the earldom of Carlisle. In its later days the house became notorious from its connection with Mrs. Cornelys, the daughter of an actor, who was born at Venice in 1723, and who, after a tarnished career in various Continental towns as a public singer, came to the King's Theatre, London, to take part in one of Gluck's operas. She took possession of Carlisle House, and projected a series of society entertainments, which proved a marvellous success. The square was blocked with the coaches and chairs of her patrons. In Taylor's "Records of my Life" it is stated she had as many as 600 persons in her saloon at one time, at two guineas per head. Foreign Ministers, many of the nobility, scions of royalty, flocked to her rooms. She spent profusely and lavishly. The decorations were superb, the entertainments magnificent, in the ceremonious and rather affected style of the period. In 1770 she was at the climax of prosperity. "Galas, masquerades, and festivals, all equally splendid, succeeded one another throughout the season" (Clinch); but after her sky-rocket ascent came the fall: fickle Fashion deserted her, and finally the house and its contents were announced in the *Gazette* for sale. The Pantheon had proved too formidable a rival. In 1785 the property was in Chancery, and Mrs. Cornelys died in the Fleet Prison in 1797. The banqueting-hall in Sutton Street, attached to

Carlisle House by a covered way, was converted into the Chapel of St. Patrick, and where masqueraders had revelled priests heard confession. This also eventually disappeared, to make way for the present church, which is such a feature of the square; it stands at the corner of Sutton Street, and bears the name of its predecessor. It was opened 1893, and its campanile reaches a height of 125 feet. Within the porch is a beautiful marble group of the dead Christ, supported by an angel. The pictures inside are exceptionally valuable and beautiful, including paintings by Vandyke, Murillo, Carlo Dolci, Paul Veronese (attributed), and many others. On the opposite side of the street Messrs. Crosse and Blackwell's factory also covers a house owning historical associations. No. 21 was the "White House," and 22, "Falconberg House," in former times. The latter was the residence of Oliver Cromwell's third daughter, Lady Falconberg, who died in 1712. Sutton Street takes its name from the county seat of the Falconbergs. In this house Sir Cloudesley Shovel's body lay in state before its interment, after having been found cast up on one of the Scilly Islands. A Spanish Ambassador was among the later residents, and afterwards the house was for a time an hotel. In the large drawing-room the ceiling was painted by Angelica Kauffmann. The Duke of Argyll, the Earl of Bradford, and Speaker Onslow, were among its tenants. This house is now the offices of Messrs. Crosse and Blackwell. The painted ceiling was carefully taken down and saved from destruction by one of the heads of the firm. The chief articles of interest remaining are a handsome overmantel in one of the private rooms of the firm, and a curious ceiling. The former is of wood, and is varnished and painted in various tones of bronze and gold. The carving upon it is very elaborate and enigmatical. The panelled ceiling has some affinity with it, but has been modernized, and is not so interesting. The front of the house remains as it was, and claims to be the only original frontage in the square.

The centre of the square, when first laid out, was occupied by a fountain surmounted by a statue of Charles II. in armour, the work of Colley Cibber. Clinch in "Soho and its Associations" mentions a document of 1748, still extant, in which are recorded the subscriptions made by the inhabitants to replace the wooden palisades round the square by iron railings. This is headed by £300 from the Duke of Portland, and among the names are those of many titled and influential people, showing that fashion had not then migrated westward. It was on the doorstep of a house in the square that De Quincey sank dying of exhaustion and starvation during his first novitiate of London life, and he was only saved by his faithful companion Ann.

PART II
PICCADILLY AND ST. JAMES'S SQUARE

Returning from Soho Square to Piccadilly Circus, we find ourselves in the parish of St. James's, Piccadilly, which takes in all the now fashionable shopping locality of Regent Street, and is bounded on the east and south by St. Anne's, Soho, and St. Martin's-in-the-Fields, and on the west by St. George's, Hanover Square.

St. James's parish was separated from St. Martin's in 1685, but before that epoch it had begun to have an existence of its own. Faithorne and Newcourt's map of London, 1658, shows us open ground from a double row of trees at Pall Mall to Piccadilly; Piccadilly is marked "from Knightsbridge unto Piccadilly Hall." Opposite the palace, at the foot of the present St. James's Street, are a few houses, including Berkshire (now Bridgewater) House, and there are a few more at the eastern extremity of Pall Mall. At the north-eastern corner of what we call the Haymarket is the "Gaming House," and at the corners adjacent one or two more buildings. This is St. James's in its earliest stage, before the tide of fashion had moved so far westward. Henry Jermyn, Earl of St Albans, in the reign of Charles II. obtained a building lease of forty-five acres in St. James's Fields and projected the square, which became the nucleus of the parish.

Piccadilly.—There is no authentic derivation for this curious name, though many fancy suggestions have been made. The most probable of these is that which connects it with the peccadilloes or ruffs worn by the gallants of Charles II.'s time. Pennant traced the name to piccadillas, turnovers or cakes which were sold at Piccadilla Hall, at the upper end of the Haymarket.

In Thomas Blount's "Glossographia" we read: "Pickadil ... the round hem or the several divisions set together about the skirt of a garment or other thing; also a kinde of stiff collar made in fashion of a Bande. Hence perhaps that famous ordinary near St. James called Peckadilly took denomination because it was then the utmost or skirt house of the suburbs that way, others say it took its name from this, that one Higgins a tailor who built it got most of his estate by Pickadilles, which in the last age were much worn in England." There seems to be no other foundation than Mr. Blount's lively imagination for "Higgins a tailor."

There is as much confusion about the first date at which the name was used as there is about its derivation. Whether the hall took its name from its situation or the district from the hall will probably ever remain in doubt.

The earliest occurrence of the name is in 1636, by which time the hall was built. The gaming-house was at a later time also known as Piccadilly, which has increased the confusion. Some writers have identified the hall and the gaming-house, but there seems to be no doubt that these were two separate buildings. The former was a private house standing at the corners of Windmill and Coventry Streets. The latter seems to have been built by Robert Baker, and sold by his widow to Colonel Panton, who built Panton Street. It was otherwise known as Shaver's Hall, and had a tennis-court and upper and lower bowling-green, and was a very fashionable place of resort. The secondary name probably emanated from the proprietor's former trade, but it is said to have stuck to the place after Lord Dunbar lost £3,000 at one sitting, when people said a Northern lord had been shaved here.

Sir John Suckling was among the habitués of the place, and his sisters will ever be remembered from Aubrey's pathetically humorous description of their coming "to the Peccadillo bowling-green crying for feare he should lose all [their] portions," as he was a great gamester.

The name Piccadilly appears to have begun at the east end, near the circus, and spread over the whole, a fact which is in favour of its being derived from the house, not the name of the house from the locality.

Regent Street is Nash's great memorial. The conception is undoubtedly fine, namely, a vast avenue to lead from Carlton House to a country mansion to be built for George IV. in Regent's Park. Nash's great idea, the combining of many separate buildings into one uniform façade, is here seen at its best. At first a lengthy colonnade supported by columns 16 feet high ran on either side of the quadrant, but this darkened the shops, so it was removed. The street is famous for its shops, which line it from end to end; it has also the merit of being wider than most of the London streets.

The part of the parish lying to the east of Regent Street is quite uninteresting except for Golden Square, which has been well described by Hatton as "not exactly in anybody's way, to or from anywhere." The square is mentioned in both "Humphrey Clinker" and "Nicholas Nickleby." Here Henry St. John, Lord Bolingbroke, lived, 1704-1708, and Mrs. Cibber in 1746. Angelica Kauffman lived in the centre house on the south side for many years. It was in the vicinity of the square that the great burial-ground for the plague-stricken dead was formed in the reign of Charles II. It was chosen as being well away from the town. Pennant says: "Golden Square, of dirty access, was built after the Revolution or before 1700. It was built by that true hero Lord Craven, who stayed in London during the whole time: and braved the fury of the pestilence with the same coolness as he fought the battles of his beloved mistress, Elizabeth, Queen of Bohemia."

It was in Golden Square that De Quincey took leave of Ann, whom he was never to see again.

Piccadilly Circus was formed at the same time as Regent Street, though it has been altered since. The Criterion Theatre and Restaurant are on the south-east side. On this site formerly stood a well-known coaching inn called the White Bear. One of Shepherd's charming sketches in the Crace Collection illustrates the courtyard of the inn. Benjamin West, afterwards P.R.A., put up here on the night of his first sojourn in London. In the centre of the circus is a fountain in memory of the seventh Earl of Shaftsbury. This was designed by Alfred Gilbert, R.A., and consists of a very light metal figure of Mercury on a very solid aluminium pedestal.

In Piccadilly itself there is the somewhat gloomy-looking geological museum, with entrance in Jermyn Street, open free to all comers. The church of St James's, which comes shortly after, was built by Sir Christopher Wren at the cost of Henry Jermyn, Earl of St. Albans, and consecrated at first as a chapel of ease to St. Martin's. The first rector was Tenison, afterwards Archbishop of Canterbury. Wren considered this one of his best works. He says: "In this church ... though very broad and the nave arched, yet there are no walls of a second order, nor lanterns, nor buttresses, but the whole roof rests upon the pillars, as do also the galleries; I think it may be found beautiful and convenient, and as such the cheapest of any form I could invent."

The church is very wide in proportion to its length, and is said to seat 2,000 people easily. The reredos, a handsome piece of wood carving with a central group of the pelican in her piety, typical of Christ giving His life's blood for fainting souls, is the work of Grinling Gibbons. The organ, in the western gallery, is supposed to have been the work of Bernard Schmidt and was built for the Roman Catholic Oratory at Whitehall, but was given to St. James's by Queen Mary, 1691.

The font which stands in the vestibule at the west end is a most excellent piece of work. It was carved from a block of white marble by Grinling Gibbons, and is about 5 feet in height. The shaft is the tree of life, round which is twined the serpent, while figures of Adam and Eve stand on either side. It is well worth going into the church to see this alone. The font originally possessed a cover, which was stolen in 1800, and is said to have been hung up in a spirit shop. In the church are many monuments hanging on the walls, and on the pillars. One or two of these at the east end are very cumbrous, and many are heavily decorated, but none are worthy of note for any intrinsic beauty they possess. Walcott notes as the most important those of the eighth Earl of Huntingdon, 1704, and Count de la Roche Foucault, 1741. James Dodsley, the well-known bookseller, 1797, was buried here, also Haysman, the rival of Lely, and Lieutenant-General Sir Colin Campbell, K.C.B., 1847.

Among the entries in the register we have the burials of the two Vanderveldes, father and son.

In the old graveyard there are stones in abundance, one or two on the wall of the church, and many alternating with the flagstones over which the feet of the living carelessly pass.

In Sackville Street, just opposite to the church, Sheridan died.

There are various other public buildings of more or less interest before we come to Burlington House. No less than three mansions stood here in the times of the later Stuarts. These belonged to Lord Chancellor Clarendon and Lords Berkeley and Burlington, of which the latter name has alone survived.

The third Earl was an architect, and added several embellishments to his mansion, including a stone frontage and a colonnade taken down in 1868.

Handel was a guest at Burlington House for three years from 1715. After the death of Lord Burlington in 1753 the title became extinct. Among the memorable scenes witnessed by the house was a brilliant ball and fête, given by the members of White's Club to the allied Sovereigns in 1814.

Lord George Cavendish, who bought the house in 1815, considerably altered the interior of the building, and built the Burlington Arcade in 1819. He was afterwards created Earl of Burlington. In 1854 Government bought the house and garden. The University of London, now in Burlington Gardens, temporarily occupied the building, and the societies occupying Somerset House were offered quarters in Burlington House. In 1866 the mansion was leased to the Royal Academy, and fundamental changes began.

On the east side of Burlington House are the Geographical and Chemical Societies, and on the west the Linnæan. In the courtyard, the Royal Society is in the east wing, and the Royal Astronomical and the Society of Antiquaries in the western.

On the site of the Albany, now fashionable "chambers" for unmarried men, were formerly three houses united into one by Lord Sunderland, the third Earl, chiefly remembered for his magnificent library, which, when the earldom of Sunderland was merged in the dukedom of Marlborough in 1733, formed the nucleus of the Blenheim Library. The brother of the great Fox held the house for a short time, and from him it passed to Lord Melbourne, to whom its rebuilding was due. The architect was Sir W. Chambers, and the ceilings decorated by Cipriani, Rebecca, and Wheatley.

It was from the Duke of York and Albany, uncle of George III., that the name is derived. However, he did not live here long.

St. James's Hall is well known for its popular concerts, which bring first-rate music within the reach of all. In St. James's Hall the first public dinner was held on June 2, 1858, and was given under the presidency of Mr. R. Stephenson, M.P., to Sir F. P. Smith in recognition of his services in introducing the screw propeller in our steam fleet. Charles Dickens gave his second series of readings here in 1861.

Passing down Duke Street, on the south side of Piccadilly, we come to Jermyn Street. Sir Walter Scott stayed at an hotel here in 1832, on his last journey home. Sir Isaac Newton was also a resident, and the poet Gray lodged here.

In King Street are Willis's Rooms, once Almack's, at one time the scene of many fashionable assemblies. The rooms were opened in 1765, and a ten-guinea subscription included a ball and supper once a week for three months. Ladies were eligible for membership, and thus the place can claim to have been one of the earliest ladies' clubs. Walpole writes in 1770 to George Montagu: "It is a club of both sexes to be erected at Almack's on the model of that of the men at White's.... I am ashamed to say I am of so young and fashionable society." The lady patronesses were of the very highest rank. Timbs quotes from a letter of Gilly Williams: "You may imagine by the sum, the company is chosen, though refined as it is, it will scarcely put old Soho [Mrs. Cornelys] out of countenance." The place steadily maintained its popularity. Captain Gronow in 1814 says: "At the present time one can hardly conceive the importance which was attached to getting admission to Almack's, the seventh heaven of the fashionable world." The large ballroom was about 100 feet in length by 40 in width, and the largest number of persons present at one time was 1,700. It is often mentioned in the contemporary fiction dealing with fashionable society; indeed, the whole of this neighbourhood was the theatre for much of the gay life of the eighteenth century.

St. James's Square is redolent of old memories. It was, as has been stated, built by Henry Jermyn, Earl of St. Albans. The square seems to have been a fashionable locality from its very foundation, and, curiously enough, has escaped the fate of so many of its compeers, and still continues aristocratic.

The workmanship of all the houses was solid and durable, and as soon as they were built they were occupied. A catalogue of the names of the early inhabitants would occupy much space: titled men, men eminent in letters, science and political life, thronged the arena. The proximity to the Court was a great attraction. The centre of the square was at first left in a neglected condition, a remnant of the "Fields" on which the houses had been built, and it served as a base for the displays of fireworks which were given after the taking of Namur and the Peace of Ryswick.

In 1726 a Bill was passed in Parliament for the cleansing and beautifying of the square, which had become a disgrace to the neighbourhood, being a mere offal-heap. An ornamental basin was constructed and the square paved, and a bronze equestrian statue of William III., clad, according to the ludicrous custom of a bygone time, in Roman habit, was erected in 1808, on a pedestal which had been built for it in the centre of the basin years before. The water in this basin is associated with at least one historic scene, for in the riots of 1780 the malcontents threw the keys of Newgate into it, where they remained undiscovered for many years. The basin was finally drained in 1840, trees were planted, and the garden laid out. Among the historic associations is one of a memorable night, when Dr. Johnson and Richard Savage paced round and round the square for lack of a lodging, and pledged each other, as they separated, to stand by their country.

Norfolk House stands on the site of that of the Earl of St. Albans, which he built for his own use in the south-east corner, he afterwards removed to the mansion on the north side. In the Earl's first house the Grand-Duke of Tuscany, afterwards Cosmo III., lodged, when on a visit to London in 1669. Frederick, Prince of Wales, rented the old house before Carlton House was prepared for his reception, and here George III. was born. The old house still stands behind the newer building.

Next to Norfolk House is London House, attached to the See of London since about 1720.

Next to this, at the south corner of Charles Street, is Derby House, with handsome iron veranda and railings running round it. It was built by Lord Bellasis, and one of the earliest occupants was Aubrey de Vere, twentieth Earl of Oxford. Dasent says there is some reason for supposing it to have been occupied by Sir Robert Walpole between the years 1732-35. It was bought by the Earl of Derby about the middle of the present century. All the houses on this side of the square are of dull brick, in formal style, with neither beauty nor originality. The next, at the northern corner of Charles Street (now the West End branch of the London and Westminster Bank), was known as Ossulston House until 1753, and belonged for a long period to the Bennet family. It covered two numbers, of which one was occupied by Lord Dartmouth, Lord Privy Seal under Lord North's Administration, and is now the bank, and the other was bought by the second Viscount Falmouth, and is now occupied by the seventh Viscount of that name.

No. 3 has passed through the hands of many titled and distinguished owners, and is at present the property of the Duke of Leeds. It was occupied by the Copyhold Inclosure and the Tithe Commission Office, now the Board of Agriculture.

No. 4, in the corner, belongs to Lord Cowper, and No. 5 to the Earl of Strafford.

The next two belong to Lord Avebury and Earl Egerton.

No. 8 has had many vicissitudes. It was for a time occupied as the French Embassy, later by Sir Cyril Wyche, President of the Royal Society, also by Monmouth's widow, Josiah Wedgwood, and by many intervening tenants of distinction. After the occupancy of Wedgwood, the second Earl of Romney was here for eight years, until 1839, and then the house became successively the home of the Erectheum Club, of the Charity Commissioners, the Junior Oxford and Cambridge Club, Vine Club, York Club, Junior Travellers' Club, and at present it is the Sports Club. Ormond or Chandos House, which took up three numbers at the west corner of York Street, has a history. It was built by Lord St. Albans in place of his first house in the south-eastern corner of the square, and passed into the possession of the Duke of Ormond, the only man who was four times Lord Lieutenant of Ireland. Entertainments on a large scale took place during this period. Perhaps the most interesting fact in the history of the house is that a meeting of noblemen and gentlemen was held here in 1688, at which an address of welcome to the Prince of Orange was drawn up, in which he was besought to carry on the Government until a Convention could meet. The Spanish Embassy was here in 1718. The Duke of Chandos bought the mansion a year later, and in 1735 it was pulled down, and the present three houses built on its site. These three houses have been well tenanted, especially the centre one, No. 10, which can boast the successive occupancy of Pitt, Lady Blessington, the great Earl of Derby, and Mr. Gladstone. Here old link-extinguishers still remain on the posts before the door.

No. 9 is now the home of the Portland Club.

No. 12 has also its string of names, but, for fear of degenerating into a mere catalogue, we will only mention a few of the most important, Sir Cyril Wyche was the first owner in 1676, and he was succeeded in 1678 by Aubrey de Vere, twentieth Earl of Oxford. The Dukes of Roxburgh were in possession from 1796 to 1812, and at the latter date the famous Roxburgh Library was sold. The last private occupier was J. W. Spencer Churchill, seventh Duke of Marlborough. After this the house was used successively by the Salisbury Club, the Nimrod Club, and the Pall Mall Club, the last of which remains here at present.

No. 13, the corner house, has passed through many hands, and is now in the occupation of the Windham Club. The London Library is well known to all book-lovers.

Wheatley states that Philip Francis lived at No. 14 until his death in 1818, but the houses have been renumbered since then, and his 14 is now 16.

No. 15 is known as Lichfield House from its former owner. It was built by Stuart (known as "Athenian Stuart") in 1763-65. In 1855 it was the home of the Junior United Service Club. In 1856 it was bought by the Clerical, Medical, and General Life Assurance Society. The chief event in its history took place on June 28, 1815, when the Prince Regent displayed the trophies and banners just brought from Waterloo to the crowd below.

No. 16, which is now amalgamated with 17, is occupied by the East India United Service Club.

Nos. 17 and 18 formed old Halifax House. Many political intrigues and meetings must have taken place here, for Lord Halifax gained the name of always being on the winning side. In 1725 Halifax House was demolished and the present buildings erected. In 1820 Queen Caroline stayed in No. 17 during her trial. The house was afterwards used by the Colonial Club.

No. 18 boasts such names among its tenants as the fourth Earl of Chesterfield, the first Lord Thurlow, and Viscount Castlereagh, afterwards second Marquis of Londonderry. It was used by the Oxford and Cambridge Club and the Army and Navy Club.

At the south-east corner of King Street, in the square, was Cleveland House, which has been demolished and replaced by "mansions."

Apsley and Winchester Houses follow. The former was rebuilt by Robert Adam in 1772-74, and follows the well-known lines of his work, with fluted pilasters rising from above the basement to an entablature. The entrance has the fan-shaped glass above the door so characteristic of Adam's work.

Winchester House was from 1826 to 1875 occupied by the Bishops of that see, and was later a branch of the War Office, several departments of which are still here. The next magnificent building, which really faces George Street, but was formerly considered to be in the square, is one of the palatial clubs evolved by the demands of modern luxury. The house which formerly stood here was used by the Parthenon Club from 1837-41, and was subsequently pulled down to make way for the present clubhouse, opened 1851, and built from designs by Parnell and Smith. The exterior is a combination of Sansovino's Palazzo Cornaro and the Library of St. Mark at Venice. The lower part follows Sansovino's beautiful work very closely. On the site of this stood formerly a house belonging to Nell Gwynne, of which

Pennant writes: "The back-room of the ground-floor was (within memory) entirely of looking-glass, as was said to have been the ceiling; over the chimney was her picture, and that of her sister in a third room." He describes this house as the "first good one on the left hand of St. James's Square entered from Pall Mall."

The south side of the square has never been held in such esteem as the remaining three-fourths. But the Junior Carlton Club, facing Pall Mall, has removed this stigma; it is a fine specimen of architecture. Demolition, previous to reconstruction, has already begun next to it. After this as far as John Street is a row of comparatively insignificant narrow houses of various heights and styles. Some of the houses on the north side of Pall Mall were built before the completion of the square, so that there was no room for large mansions here. At the corner of John Street and Pall Mall is what is called "Ye Olde Bull Tavern," a square box-like stuccoed house. This is probably contemporary with the first building of Pall Mall, and may have been the substitute of the seventeenth century wits and men of letters for the magnificent clubs of the present day.

Charles Street was built about 1671, and was, of course, named after the King. Burke and Canning are numbered among the former residents.

York Street was named in compliment to the Duke of York, afterwards James II. It may be noted that the four streets surrounding the square form the names King Charles and Duke of York.

Bury Street was named after a Mr. Berry, who was landlord of many of the houses; the spelling is a corruption. Sir Richard Steele lodged here, also Thomas Moore and Crabbe, the poet, during one of his later visits to London, when contact with cultured men had rubbed off his early boorishness.

"St. James's Street is much more remarkable for the natural advantages and beauty of the ground, than from any addition it has received from art," so says Ralph ("Critical Review of Public Buildings," 1783 edition). In the very earliest maps of the parish a road is marked on this site, leading northward from the palace. The street was built about 1670, and was first known as Long Street. In the time of the Stuarts it shared the aristocratic tendency of the square, and had a list of noble occupiers. It was levelled and made uniform in 1764, having previously descended from Piccadilly by steps.

St. James's Street has been noted from the very beginning for its clubs, gaming-houses, and convivial gatherings. Its proximity to the Court attracted all the fops and beaux, and it was the resort of fashionable and gay young idlers. Many anecdotes are related of the street, but chiefly in connection with the clubs, for which it is still famous. White's (37 and 38) is one of the oldest; it was established about 1698, and was at first a chocolate-house. It stood near the low end of the street, on the west side. It was burnt down in 1733, and the present building, designed by Wyatt, was erected in 1755, and altered nearly a century later by Lockyer. The gaming-room of the old house forms the scene of the sixth plate of Hogarth's "Rake's Progress," where the gamblers are represented intent on their cards, though the flames are bursting out. It was after the fire that the house became a private club, and it was long noted as a gambling-house for high stakes and reckless betting. It is of White's that the story is told that a man dropped down before the door insensible, and was taken inside. The members immediately began to bet whether he were dead or not, and when the physician came to bleed him, those on the affirmative side protested.

"Brooke's" is now No. 60, on the opposite side of the street from White's, at the northern corner of Park Place, and was as notorious a gaming-house as White's. It was of later origin, dating from 1764, and was originally in Pall Mall. It began life under the name of Almack's. The play was prodigiously high. Timbs says that it was for rouleaux of £50 each, and there was generally £10,000 in specie on the table.

"Boodle's," is another celebrated club, which was also named the "Savoir Vivre." This is now No. 28.

The Cocoa-tree Club recalls by its name an old chocolate house of Queen Anne's time, a favourite resort of the Tories, often mentioned by Addison. Lord Byron was one of the members. The old house was situated nearer to the south end of the street than the present club.

"Arthurs," south of St. James's Place, was founded by the proprietor of White's in 1765. The present building was erected in 1825 by Hopper. The Conservative Club house (74) was built in 1845 from designs by Smirke and Basevi. The building is large, with slightly projecting wings, and a stone balcony extending uninterruptedly across the frontage.

Next door is the "Thatched House" Club, which originated in the Thatched House Tavern, in which the dilettanti and literary societies used to meet. Wheatley describes a row of low-built shops standing before the tavern, one of which was that of the hairdresser Rowland, who made a fortune by his macassar oil.

St. James's Coffee-house, a celebrated Whig rendezvous from the reign of Queen Anne until the beginning of the nineteenth century, was at this end of the street. In this street there are also many other clubs of later origin. It was at the foot of St. James's Street that the Duke of Ormond was attacked in his coach in 1670, by the notorious Colonel Blood. The Duke had been responsible for the execution of some of Blood's associates in Ireland, and

Blood determined to take him to Tyburn and hang him in revenge. He actually succeeded in dragging him from his coach and mounting him on horseback behind one of his men. When they had proceeded as far as Devonshire House, the Duke succeeded in unhorsing his companion, and in the delay that followed his servants made their appearance and rescued him. For this outrage Blood was never punished. Sir Christopher Wren died in St. James's Street in 1723, and Gibbon, the historian, in 1794. The names of Waller, the poet, Wolfe, C. Fox, and Lord Byron, are among the residents. It was here that the last named was lodging when his "Childe Harold" created such an extraordinary sensation. Alexander Pope was also a resident.

McLean, the famous highwayman, lodged opposite "White's." He was hung in 1750, and the first Sunday after he was condemned 3,000 people went to see him in gaol. St. James's Street at present is sufficiently noticeable because of its width, in which the old palace gateway at the foot is framed.

Park Place was built in 1683. William Pitt came to live here in 1801. St. James's Place is a medley of old and modern buildings, some having been built in the last decade. Wheatley speaks of it because of its tortuous course, as "one of the oddest built streets in London." Wilkes and Addison, and Mrs. Delaney, at whose house Miss Burney stayed, have been among the residents. Samuel Rogers lived for fifty years at No. 22, which looked out over the park.

Cleveland Square is an open space before the Duke of Bridgewater's House. The house was restored, as an inscription over the doorway tells us, or in other words rebuilt, in 1849. This house has a history. It was originally Berkshire House, and belonged to the Howards, Earls of Berkshire. Charles II. bought it in 1670, and gave it to that "beautiful fury," Barbara, Duchess of Cleveland. She pulled down the house and sold part of the site before rebuilding. In 1730 the first Duke of Bridgewater bought it, and it was alternately known by the names of Cleveland and Bridgewater. The third Duke died unmarried in 1803, when the title became extinct. He left the house and the magnificent collection of pictures to his nephew, the Marquis of Stafford, afterwards Duke of Sutherland, with reversion to the Marquis's second son. This son was created Earl of Ellesmere in 1846. He rebuilt the house, still retaining the old name. The famous collection of pictures within, includes works of Raphael, Titian, Vandervelde, Turner, Rembrandt, Cuyp, and others, and is one of the finest private collections in England.

The house opposite was the home of Grenville, First Lord of the Admiralty in 1806, and here he collected the magnificent library which is now at the British Museum. Admiral Rodney lived in Cleveland Row in 1772.

On Pall Mall the game of the same name was originally played. On both sides of the open space were rows of elm-trees. But being such an obvious route from the palace to Charing Cross it was soon used as a thoroughfare, and after the warrant for "building of the new street of St. James" Charles II. laid out the new mall in the park. The street, when built, was at first called Catherine, in honour of the Queen, but the older name soon returned into favour.

It early became fashionable. Nell Gwynne was one of the first residents. She had a house numbered 79, near the War Office, afterwards, by the irony of fate, occupied by the Society for the Propagation of the Gospel, and since rebuilt. Evelyn records an occasion on which he attended King Charles II. in the park, when he heard "a familiar discourse between the King and Mrs. Nellie as they call an impudent comedian, she looking out of her garden on a terrace at the top of the wall, and the King standing on the green walk under it."

During Wyatt's insurrection in 1554, the mob passed along this road, and the Earl of Pembroke planted artillery on the high ground of Hay Hill and Piccadilly, when a piece of the Queen's ordnance, we are told, "slew three of Wyatt's followers, in a rank, and after carrying off their heads passed through this wall into the park" (Jesse). In 1682 Thynne was murdered at the instigation of Count Konigsmarck in what is now Pall Mall East, because he had married the heiress of the Percys, whom the Count wished to marry himself. The principal was acquitted, but his three accomplices or tools, who had actually committed the murder, were executed, according to the poetic justice of the time, at the scene of their offence, in 1682.

The Star and Garter Hotel, nearly opposite the War Office, was a fashionable tavern in the time of Queen Anne. Here took place the famous duel between the fifth Lord Byron and Mr. Chaworth in 1765. They fought in the house by the light of only a single candle. Byron killed his opponent, and was found guilty of manslaughter by his peers. However, he claimed benefit of a statute of Edward VI., and was discharged. The original dispute was merely as to which gentleman had the larger amount of game on his estate.

Among other famous taverns in this street are mentioned the King's Arms, under the Opera Colonnade in Pall Mall East. Also the Rumpsteak Club, which consisted of five Dukes, one Marquis, fifteen Earls, three Viscounts, and three Barons, all in opposition to Sir Robert Walpole. The King's Head, the George, the Smyrna Coffee-house, Giles' Coffee-house, Hercules Pillars, and the Tree, were among the ancient places of resort in this street—a foreshadowing of the palatial mansions of Clubland.

The north side of the street is the poorer of the two. Beginning at the western end on the south side, we have the New Oxford and Cambridge Club, the Guards, and the Oxford and Cambridge University Clubs. The first of these has a very massive entrance; the house has only a north aspect, the windows at the back being glazed with ground-glass so as not to overlook Marlborough House. A little further on is an old red-brick house with a portico on which is a female figure in bas-relief with palette and brushes. This is in great contrast to its neighbours; it is what remains (centre and west wing) of Schomberg House, built about the middle of the seventeenth century. The first Schomberg came over in the train of William of Orange; he was Count in his own country, bore several French titles, and was created an English Duke. He was killed at the Battle of the Boyne. The house was later occupied by Cumberland of Culloden, George III.'s uncle, and subsequently by Astley the painter. Astley divided it into three parts, reserving the centre for his own use. Among the tenants who succeeded him we find the names of Cosway, Paine the bookseller, and Nathaniel Hone. In the western wing Gainsborough lived, so the building has every right to its distinguishing panel of palette and brushes. During Gainsborough's occupancy everyone of wealth, beauty or fashion in the society of the day resorted here to have their features immortalized. This house is now part of the War Office, which, in a previous stage of its career, was the Ordnance Office.

The entrance to the War Office stands back behind a courtyard in which is a statue of Lord Herbert of Lea. The War Office was originally at the Horse Guards, and since its removal has gradually extended its premises by absorbing one house after another. We now come to a long series of clubs. The Carlton is rich in ornament, with polished granite columns decorating a front of Caen stone. The design was by Sydney Smirke, and is said to be founded on that of a Venetian palace. It contrasts with its neighbour, the Reform, which presents a breadth of plain surface broken only by little pediments over the windows. This was the work of Sir Charles Barry, and was copied from the Farnese Palace at Venice, of which the upper storey was the work of Michael Angelo. It is a dull, heavy-looking piece of work. On part of its site stood the house of Angerstein, a Russian merchant, whose collection of pictures formed the nucleus of our National Gallery.

The Travellers', next door, also the work of Barry, is in an Italian style. One of the rules of this club is that no person shall be eligible for membership who shall not have travelled out of the British Isles at least 500 miles in a direct line from London.

The Athenæum is one of the most princely of clubs. It was established in 1823, and the present house was built about half a dozen years later. Decimus Burton was the architect, and his work is Grecian, with a frieze copied from the famous procession in the Parthenon. The recently-added storey has been the subject of much criticism. Among those present at the preliminary meeting we find the names of Sir Humphrey Davy, Sir Francis Chantrey, Sir Thomas Lawrence, the Earl of Aberdeen, Sir Walter Scott, Thomas Moore and Faraday. Theodore Hook was one of the most popular members.

At the corner of Pall Mall East and Waterloo Place is the United Service Club built by Nash. It was instituted after the Battle of Waterloo, and was at first at the corner of Charles Street, on the site of the Junior Club of the same name.

The Guards' Monument, in Waterloo Place, was put up in 1859 in memory of the Crimea. Three figures of guardsmen—Grenadier, Coldstream, and Fusilier—in full marching uniform, stand round a granite pedestal, on which are inscribed the names of the famous Crimean battles; a pile of Russian guns actually brought from Sebastopol completes the group.

The Church of St. Philip, on the west side of Lower Regent Street, is a quaint building with Doric portico and curious little cupola, the latter a copy of the Lanthorn of Demosthenes at Athens. It was built in 1820 by Repton, from designs by Sir W. Chambers, and has the merit of being almost continually open for prayer and meditation.

On the east side the most important building is the Junior United Service Club, erected in 1852 by Nelson and James.

Market Street and St. James's Market recall the market held "west of the Haymarket, mid-way between Charles and Jermyn Street." This originated in a fair held in St. James's Fields, before the square was built, and from which Mayfair partly derives its name. This fair was suppressed on account of disorder in 1651, but revived again, and was not finally stopped until the end of Charles II.'s reign. After having been suppressed in the Fields in 1664, it was held in the market. Strype describes this market as "a large place, with a commodious market-house in the midst filled with butchers' shambles; besides the stalls in the market-place for country butchers, higglers and the like, being a market now grown to great account, and much resorted unto as being served with good provisions." In a house at the corner of Market Street lived Hannah Lightfoot, said to have been married to King George III. when Prince of Wales. The market belonged to Lord St. Albans, whose name is preserved in St. Albans Place, which ends in a foot-passage leading into Charles Street.

The Haymarket derives its name from a market for hay and straw which was held here until 1830, and was then transferred to Cumberland Market, Regent's Park, where it still continues. The market naturally involved many taverns in its neighbourhood, and the street was lined with them. The names of some were Black Horse, White Horse, Nag's Head, Cock, Phœnix, Unicorn, and Blue Posts. The theatre and the old opera-house were the most important buildings in the Haymarket. The latter was on the site of Her Majesty's Theatre and the Carlton Hotel. It was called at different times the Queen's Theatre, the King's Theatre, and Her Majesty's Theatre, so the new name is but a revival of the old. The first theatre on this site was begun in 1703 as a theatre for Betterton's famous company, which had been performing in Lincoln's Inn Fields. Operas were subsequently performed here; in fact, nearly all Handel's operas were written for this theatre. Masquerades were held in the opera-house in 1749 and 1766, and were attended by all the rank and fashion of the day, and even by royalty in disguise. In 1789 the theatre was burnt down. It was rebuilt and completed only three years after the catastrophe. This house saw some fine performances of the Italian Opera Company, and in it the names of Grisi, Rubini, Tamburini, Lablache, Mario, and Jenny Lind, first became known to the public. In 1867 it also was burnt down. For about a quarter of a century a third theatre stood here, but had no success, and was pulled down. The present theatre is of great magnificence, and will seat between 1,600 and 1,700 persons. The Haymarket Theatre opposite is dwarfed by the proximity of its gorgeous neighbour. The names of Fielding, Cibber, Macklin, and Foote are connected with various attempts to make the earliest venture on this site pay. Mozart performed here in 1765, when only eight years old. In 1820 the present building was erected by Nash, adjacent to the old theatre. The Haymarket in the last century was a great place for shows and entertainments.

In James's Street was a tennis-court much patronized by Charles II. and the Duke of York.

Whitcomb Street was formerly called Hedge Lane, an appropriate name when it stood in a rural district; now it is a narrow, dirty thoroughfare, bordered by poor dwellings and small shops.

PART III
THE STRAND

We have now made a circuit, noting all that is interesting by the way, and have returned to busy Charing Cross, from which runs the great thoroughfare, the Strand, which gives the district its name.

This important street might be considered either as a street of palaces—and in this respect not to be surpassed by any street in medieval Europe, not even Venice—or a street full of associations, connected chiefly with retail trade, taverns, shops, sedan-chairs, and hackney coaches.

The Strand, as the name implies, was the shore by the river. It has passed through two distinct phases. First, when it was an open highway, with a few scattered houses here and there, crossed by small bridges over the rivulets which flowed down to the Thames. One of these was the Strand Bridge, between the present Surrey Street and Somerset House; another, Ivy Bridge, between Salisbury Street and Adam Street. In 1656 there were more than 800 watercourses crossing it between Palace Yard and the Old Exchange! It was not paved until Henry VIII.'s reign, and we read of the road being interrupted with thickets and bushes.

Then came a period of great grandeur, when the Strand was lined with palatial mansions, which had gardens stretching down to the river, when the town-houses of the Prince-Bishops, of the highest nobility, and even of royalty, rose up in grandeur. The names of the streets, Salisbury and Buckingham, York and Durham, Norfolk and Exeter, are no mere fancy, but recall a vision of bygone splendour which might well cause the Strand to be named a street of palaces.

The palaces, which occupied at one time the whole of the south side of the street, were at first the town-houses of the Bishops. They were built along the river because, in their sacred character, they were safe from violence (except in one or two cases), and therefore did not need the protection of the wall, while it was perhaps felt that even if the worst happened, as it did happen in Jack Straw's rebellion, the river offered a liberally safe way of escape. In the thirteenth century Henry III. gave Peter of Savoy "all those houses in the Thames on the way called the Strand."

Gay speaks of the change that had fallen upon the Strand in his time:

"Through the long Strand together let us stray;
With thee conversing I forget the way.

Behold that narrow street which steep descends,
Whose building to the shining shore extends;
Here Arundel's fam'd structure rear'd its frame,
The street alone retains an empty name:
Where Titian's glowing paint the canvas warm'd,
And Raphael's fair design with judgment charm'd,
Now hangs the bellman's song, and pasted here
The colour'd prints of Overton appear;
Where statues breath'd the work of Phidias' hands,
A wooden pump or lonely watch-house stands;
There Essex's stately pile adorn'd the shore,
There Cecil's, Bedford's, Villiers's—now no more."

Disraeli, in "Tancred," says: "The Strand is, perhaps, the finest street in Europe." Charles Lamb said: "I often shed tears in the motley Strand for fulness of joy at so much life."

The Strand has now become a street of shops instead of a street of palaces; it has been, but is no more, a fashionable resort; it has been a place for the lodgings of visitors, and still has many small hotels and boarding-houses in its riverside lanes; its personal associations are many, but not so important as those in the City or Westminster; it is a street of great interest, but its architectural glories have almost all vanished.

Beginning at the west end, we note on the north side the Golden Cross Hotel, rebuilt. This is the successor of a famous old coaching inn, which stood further west. On the south side is Craven Street, formerly Spur Alley, where once Benjamin Franklin lived at No. 7. The site of Hungerford Market is now covered by the Charing Cross railway-station. In Charing Cross station-yard is a modern reproduction of the original Queen Eleanor's Cross. The market was built in 1680, rebuilt in 1831, and stretched to the river. The name will always be connected with that of Charles Dickens, and with "David Copperfield." Beside the market was the suspension bridge constructed by Brunel, opened in 1845, and removed to make room for the railway-bridge.

On the site of Hungerford Market there stood the "Inn" or House of the Bishop of Norwich. In 1536 Charles Brandon, Duke of Suffolk, exchanged his house in Southwark for this place; twenty years later it fell into the hands of Heath, Archbishop of York, who called it York House, and in the reign of James I. it became the property of the Crown. Bacon was born in this house. In 1624 the Duke of Buckingham obtained the house; he pulled it down, and began to build a large mansion to take its place. The watergate is the only part of his structure still existing. Cromwell gave the house to Fairfax, whose daughter married the second Duke of Buckingham, of the

Villiers family. In 1655 Evelyn describes the house as "much ruined through neglect." In 1672 the house and gardens were sold to four persons of Westminster, who laid out the site in streets, viz., Villiers Street, Duke Street, Buckingham Street, and Of Alley, forming in conjunction the words Villiers, Duke of Buckingham. York House was pulled down soon after, and York Buildings erected on the site. Peter the Great had lodgings in York Buildings during his visit to England, and Pepys occupied a house on the west side, near the river, for some time. The gardens of the Victoria Embankment now fill up the space over which the river formerly flowed, and the watergate is merely a meaningless ornament 100 yards or more from the water.

At the corner of Agar and King William Streets, on the north, is the Charing Cross Hospital, founded 1818, and built on the present site in 1831, the architect being Decimus Burton. It is a dreary stuccoed building, with a rounded end, and contains nothing that specially marks it out from other general hospitals.

In Chandos Street the highwayman Claude Duval was arrested, after which he was executed at Tyburn, 1669. There was an ancient hostelry called the Black Prince in Chandos Street, which is mentioned by Dickens. This was demolished to make way for the Medical College. Opposite was the blacking shop where Dickens spent a miserable part of his childhood.

The next group of streets on the south side, namely, John, Robert, James, and William Streets, was built by four brothers of the name of Adam, who gave their Christian names to their handiwork, and from whom this particular district was called the "Adelphi," from the Greek word signifying brothers. The site was occupied by Durham House, a palace built by Anthony de Beck, Bishop of Durham in Edward I.'s reign. Bishop Tunstall in 1535 exchanged it with Henry VIII. for Cold Harbour and other houses in the City, and for a time it was frequented by royalty. The King gave a great tournament here on his marriage with Anne of Cleves. Proclamations of the jousts were made in France, Spain, Scotland, and Flanders. The young King, Edward VI., granted the house to his sister Elizabeth for life. The unfortunate Lady Jane Grey was married within the walls of Durham House to the son of Northumberland. When Queen Mary ascended the throne, she gave the palace back to Bishop Tunstall, but Elizabeth regarded it as one of the royal palaces, and after her accession bestowed it on Sir Walter Raleigh. In Aubrey's "Letters" Raleigh's occupation of the house is mentioned in a descriptive passage: "Durham House was a noble palace.... I well remember his (Raleigh's) study, which was on a little turret that looked into and over the Thames, and had the prospect which is, perhaps, as pleasant as any in the world." When Raleigh was imprisoned the See of Durham again obtained the house. The stables, facing the Strand, were then in a very ruinous condition, and were pulled down. On their site was built an exchange, called the New Exchange, which obtained some popularity. This was erected partly on the pattern of the Royal Exchange, and was opened by King James I. This, Strype tells us, "was for milliners, sempstresses, and other trades that furnish dresses."

The place was opened in 1609 by James I. and the Queen; it was called Britain's Burse. It became fashionable after the Restoration, and, after a period of popularity lasting a little more than fifty years, it was taken down. Here Anne Clarges, daughter of John Clarges, a farrier of the Savoy, sold gloves, washballs, and powder. She married General Monk, and died Duchess of Albemarle. Here Henry Herringman, publisher, had his shop. The Restoration literature abounds in references to the New Exchange. The shops were served by girls who spent a great part of their time in flirting with the fops. The Duchess of Tyrconnell, sister of Sarah, Duchess of Marlborough, is said to have kept a shop here for her own maintenance, wearing a white mask which she never removed. The lower walk was a notorious place for assignations. It was taken down in 1737. In 1768 the brothers Adam obtained the lease of the ground and began to build. Robert Adam had been much struck in his foreign travels with the palace of Diocletian on the Bay of Spalatro. The terrace facing the sea had impressed his imagination, and the Adelphi Terrace is the result of his adaptation of the idea. It was necessary to gain a solid foundation on the slippery river-bank, therefore the brothers designed the wonderful system of arches on which all the Adelphi precinct rests. On building their terrace they had to encroach on the river, and form an embankment, which was much resented by the Londoners. The centre house in the terrace was taken by Garrick, who remained there until his death, about seven years later. The arches were at first left open, but formed a refuge for the vicious and destitute, who made a regular city of the underground passages. They were subsequently filled in, and now are brewers' vaults, with only the high-vaulted roadway left open to form a passage for the drays and vans. Beneath the terrace is a curious little strip of land cut off from the Embankment garden by high wooden pales. This is practically useless, as it can only be reached through the arches. On it is an old dilapidated shed, once a much-frequented tavern, called the Fox under the Hill, a curious feature on land which is of so much value.

There are several interesting houses in the Adelphi precinct. In the centre of the terrace is the Savage Club, and there are many other societies and institutions on the terrace. In John Street is the building expressly designed for the Society of Arts.

The work of the Society is brought before the notice of the public by circular tablets, which are affixed to houses in London which have formerly been the homes of men eminent in literature, science, or art. Close at hand is the bank of Messrs. Coutts, on the site of the New Exchange. This important bank deserves some special notice. It was established by a goldsmith of the name of Middleton, who kept a shop near St. Martin's Church about 1692. The name of Coutts first appears in 1755. Many interesting stories are told in connection with this famous house. The Mr. Coutts who was head of the firm at the beginning of the present century was twice married. By his first wife he had three daughters, who married respectively the third Earl of Guilford, the first Marquess of Bute, and Sir Francis Burdett. His second wife was Miss Mellon, an actress, to whom he left the whole of his vast fortune. She afterwards married the Duke of St. Albans, but left the whole of her great wealth to Miss Angela Burdett, grand-daughter of Mr. Coutts. This lady assumed the additional name of Coutts, and was raised to the peerage on account of her munificent charities.

The Adelphi Theatre stands on the north side of the Strand, but is identified by name with this district; it was originally called the Sans Pareil. Charles Mathews gave many of his celebrated "at homes" here. A few doors west is the Vaudeville.

Ivy Bridge Lane, now closed, runs to the west of Salisbury Street. It is a narrow, dirty passage, and was named from a bridge in the Strand which crossed one of the numerous rivulets running down to the Thames. Pennant mentions a house of the Earl of Rutland's near this bridge. The Cecil Hotel is built over Salisbury and Cecil Streets, names that recall a mansion of Sir Robert Cecil, second son of Lord Burleigh, called Salisbury House.

Adjacent to this stood Worcester House. It was originally the town-house of the Bishops of Carlisle; at the Reformation it was presented to the Earl of Bedford, and known as Bedford House, until the owner built another house on the north side of the Strand. It then became the property of the Marquis of Worcester, and was known as Worcester House. Lord Clarendon lived here after the Restoration. At Worcester House his daughter Anne was married to the Duke of York. Lord Clarendon left the house, and went to live in St. James's Street. Worcester House was then used for great occasions.

Here the Duke of Ormond (1669) was installed Chancellor of the University of Oxford, and in 1674 the Duke of Monmouth Chancellor of the University of Cambridge. The Worcester House Conference was also held in the hall of this place. Beaufort Buildings occupy a part of the site. The house itself was destroyed by the Duke of Beaufort.

Exeter Street and Hall (north) preserve the name of Exeter House, built by Lord Burleigh. It was at first Cecil House, but on the succession of his eldest son, the Earl of Exeter, elder brother of Sir Robert Cecil, it became Exeter House. Afterwards the house was used by Doctors of Ecclesiastical Law, etc., and later was converted into an exchange, at first designed for the sale of fancy goods, but later famous for an exhibition of wild beasts. The body of Gay the poet rested in this Exchange before being interred in Westminster Abbey.

Exeter Hall was erected in 1830 for the purpose of religious meetings. Exeter Street will always be associated with the name of Dr. Johnson, who took lodgings here when he came up to London first, and dined at a neighbouring cookshop for eightpence.

The Lyceum Theatre was designed by S. Beazley, and opened in 1834. It will be always associated with the names of Sir Henry Irving and Ellen Terry. It stands on the site of the English Opera-House, burnt down in 1830, which during many years was the home of a quaint convivial gathering, called the Beefsteak Society, founded by Rich and Lambert in 1735. The members dined together off beefsteaks at five o'clock on Saturdays from November until the end of June. The gridiron was their emblem.

Just before arriving at Wellington Street there is a glimpse of green trees, and of a brilliant bed of flowers, down a little narrow street on the south side of the Strand. Many people must have noticed these things, few have had the curiosity to explore further; yet it is well worth while to get down from omnibus or cab and venture into this little backwater of the Savoy. Between eleven and one, and two and four o'clock every day the garden gate is open, and the verger is in the chapel, ready to answer questions. The little graveyard garden, with its waving trees, is a veritable oasis in the desert of brick and mortar, and the quaint chapel with its turret forms a suitable background. The precincts of the Savoy appertain to the Duchy of Lancaster, and as such are royal property; the reigning Sovereign keeps up the place, and pays for choir and service. In former days many irregular marriages were performed here, until the place gained a reputation second only to the Fleet Prison. Weddings are still held here, though the procedure is now strictly legal. The origin of the church was in the reign of Henry VII., but the fire which raged in 1864, and burnt out the interior, destroyed many old relics, and the present interior is Early Victorian. There is a curious old oil-painting opposite the door, which looks as if it had been part of a triptych, and in the chancel two quaint little stone figures, which survived the fire. The latest stained-glass window was filled in quite recently in memory of D'Oyley Carte. It was unveiled by Sir Henry Irving in the spring of 1902. Several persons of importance have been buried here, but none whose names are sufficiently well known to merit quotation. Many Bishops have been consecrated in the chapel, and it was here that the memorable Conference on the Book of Common Prayer took place in Charles II.'s reign. The chapel was made parochial after the greedy Somerset had destroyed the first Church of St. Mary le Strand, in order to use its materials for his own mansion. It had before that time been dedicated to St. John the Baptist, but was henceforth known as St. Mary le Savoy.

The history of the precinct of Savoy is difficult to treat in a volume like the present, because it requires a book to itself. It is not the paucity of material, but the quantity, that is embarrassing. The great palace which stood here first was built by Simon de Montfort, Earl of Leicester, one of the Barons to whom our present Constitution is due. By one of the frequent vicissitudes of the times, when no man's land or property was safe, this palace came into the hands of King Henry III., who took the opportunity of a visit from his wife's uncle, Peter of Savoy (afterwards Earl of Savoy and Richmond), to present it to him. Peter either gave it to or exchanged it with a religious fraternity, from whom it was rebought by the Queen, Eleanor, who gave it to her son Edmund, Earl of Lancaster.

After the Battle of Poitiers, King John of France was brought here a prisoner, and, oddly enough, though he was soon set at liberty, his death occurred here many years later when he had returned to make amends for the escape of one of his sons held hostage by the English until the payment of his ransom.

John of Gaunt, Duke of Lancaster, had made the palace into a most magnificent building, and here he lived in great state. Chaucer, Froissart and Wycliff are mentioned as having been his frequent guests. In the sack of the town by Wat Tyler this house particularly attracted the attention of the unruly mob, who did their utmost to wreck it, and were assisted by the explosion of several barrels of gunpowder, which, ignorant of their contents, they had thrown upon the flames. The costly plate and rich furniture were flung into the Thames by the rioters. After this it lay in ruins until King Henry VII., himself a descendant of John of Gaunt, founded here a hospital for 100 poor people, but he hardly lived to see his project carried out. Amid the general spoliation of the religious houses that followed, Henry VIII. seems to have respected his father's wish and left the hospital alone. It is described as a goodly building in the form of a cross. However, it was suppressed under Edward VI., and restored by Mary, whose maids of honour "did with exemplary piety furnish it with all necessaries." Elizabeth laid hands on it, and later it seems to have been reserved for such nobles as had the favour of the Crown and the right of free quarters, something in the same way as Hampton Court is reserved at present. There is an illustration by Hollar showing the palace-hospital as it was in 1650. It is right on the water's edge, presenting a very solid line of wall to the river, pierced by two rows of small windows. In the upper stories the parapet is battlemented, and a square tower built over arches projects from the frontage. We have also a plan of about a hundred years later (1754), showing the congeries of buildings that then covered the precincts. The part near the river is marked "Dwellings"; the ancient hospital has become "barracks." There is a military prison at the west side, and churches of the German Calvinist, German Lutheran and French persuasions are all within the walls.

The present church in this plan is at the north-west end, and all the above-mentioned buildings are to the south and east of it, covering ground now devoted to offices and mansions. A good deal of the buildings was standing even at the beginning of the nineteenth century, when it was demolished to make way for the approaches to Waterloo Bridge.

At the east corner of what is now Wellington Street stood Wimbledon House, built by Sir Edward Cecil, son to the first Earl of Exeter. It was burned down in 1628.

The great palace called Somerset House was at first built by the Protector Somerset, brother of Jane Seymour. He cleared away to make room for it the palace of the Bishops of Worcester and Chester, the Strand Inn belonging to the Temple, and many other buildings. The cloister on the north side of St. Paul's containing the "Dance of Death" was demolished in order to find stones for the new building, which was unfinished when the Protector was beheaded in 1552. The architect is supposed to have been John of Padua. It is not, however, certain how far the place was completed at the death of the Protector. Elizabeth gave the keeping of the house to her kinsman, Lord Hunsdon. James called it Denmark House. Charles gave it to his Queen, Henrietta Maria, and built a chapel for the Roman Catholic service. Some of the Queen's attendants are buried here; their tombs are in vaults under the great square. A register of the marriages, baptisms and burials which have taken place at Somerset House has been published by Sir T. Philips. Here Henrietta appeared in a masque; here died Inigo Jones; here Oliver Cromwell's body lay in state; after the Restoration Henrietta returned here for a time; Catherine of Braganza succeeded; here the body of Monk, Duke of Albemarle, lay in state; and here, after Catherine left England, the place became like the Savoy, the favoured residence of the poorer nobility. The old building was destroyed in 1775.

In the new Somerset House, erected 1776-1786—architect, Sir William Chambers—were for many years held the meetings of the Royal Society; the Society of Antiquaries; the Royal Academy of Arts; the Astronomical,

Geological and Geographical Societies. A great deal of public business is carried on at Somerset House. The east wing is occupied by King's College, founded in 1828. Opposite to Somerset House a stream came down from the higher ground; it was crossed by the Strand Bridge. The waters flowed through the palace into the river.

On the east side of Somerset House stood Arundel House, originally Bath's Inn, as the town-house of the Bishop of Bath and Wells. In this house were set up the famous Arundel marbles. The Duc de Sully, who was lodged here during his embassy to England on the accession of James I., speaks of it as a most commodious house. Near Arundel House and Somerset House was an Inn of Chancery called Chester Inn.

Among the buildings destroyed to make room for Somerset House was a small church dedicated to the Virgin Mary, and, according to some, to St. Ursula. The Duke of Somerset promised to build another for the people, but was beheaded before he could fulfil his promise. On the present site of St. Mary's Church, and at the west end, stood a stone cross where the justices itinerant sat at certain seasons, and also on the site was the old Strand well. The cross became decayed, and a maypole was erected either on its site or close beside it. The Puritans pulled down the maypole, but after the Restoration another and a much taller one, measuring in two pieces 134 feet, was put up by sailors under the direction of the Duke of York amid the rejoicings of the people. The maypole stood until 1713, when the remaining portion was carried away to Wanstead Park, where it was used for holding a telescope. The Church of St. Mary le Strand was built 1714-1723 by James Gibbs. It was the first of the fifty new churches ordered (not all built) by Queen Anne, and it was at first called New Church. The style of the church has been vehemently abused, and yet it has grown in favour and has now many admirers. It is divided into two parts, of which the lower has no window, being built solid to keep out the noise of the street. The windows are in the upper part. The church within is nobly ornamented and is without galleries. Before the west end of the church was the first stand for hackney coaches.

"Around that area side they take their stand,
Where the tall maypole o'erlooked the Strand;
And now—so Anne and Piety ordain—
A church collects the saints of Drury Lane."

And again the poet asks:

"What's not destroyed by Time's devouring hand?
Where's Troy—and where's the Maypole in the Strand?"

Mrs. Inchbald lived by the side of the New Church in the Strand.

The immense changes taking place in the Strand begin to be very noticeable opposite Somerset House. At the time of writing a few houses at the corner of Wellington Street are still standing, but will soon disappear.

On the south side of the Strand, just beyond the east end of St. Mary's Church, is a narrow entry called Strand Lane. This was formerly Strand Bridge, over one of the rivulets running down to the Thames, and later it still retained the same name, meaning the bridge or landing stairs at the river end.

Some way down this lane there is a notice pointing out a Roman bath which is still in existence and well worth seeing. The bath now belongs to Messrs. Glave, drapers in New Oxford Street, and is open free of charge for anyone to inspect between eleven and twelve o'clock on Saturday mornings. It is a rough vaulted chamber which has wisely been left without any attempt at decoration, and the bath itself measures about six yards by one and a half. It is four feet in depth, and is fed by a spring which continually flows in. Subscribers are allowed to use it on the payment of two guineas per annum. There was formerly a companion bath quite near, but this was done away with at the building of the Norfolk Hotel. The slabs of white marble which form the pavement of the existing bath were taken from it. It is curious that such a relic, computed to be perhaps 2,000 years old, should survive hidden and almost unnoticed, where so many buildings long anterior in date have utterly vanished. The bath is not mentioned by Stow or Malcolm in their accounts of London, and probably was not discovered when they wrote.

In Surrey Street Congreve died in 1729. The greater part of this and the neighbouring streets has been very recently rebuilt. Huge modern red-brick mansions with all the latest conveniences of electric light and lifts replace the old mansion which once stood here. These are carefully built and not unpicturesque; they are let in flats, and house a multitude of offices, clubs, etc. They are called by the names of the noble families who once lived here—Arundel House, Mowbray House, and Howard House. In Norfolk Street there are hotels and a small ladies' club, the Writers', the only women's club in London which demands a professional qualification from its members. Peter the Great lodged in this street, and William Penn, the Quaker, was at the last house in the south-west corner.

In Howard Street Mrs. Bracegirdle, the actress, once lodged, and a wild attempt was made by an admirer to carry her off one night as she returned from the theatre. The well-known duellist, Lord Mohun, took part in the outrage which ended in the death of the actor Mountford. Congreve was also a resident in Howard Street, removing afterwards to Surrey Street. The old Crown and Anchor Tavern stood in Arundel Street, in which was the Whittington Club, founded by Douglas Jerrold, who was the first president. At the corner of Arundel Street is the depot of W. H. Smith and Sons, the largest book and newspaper business in the world, having the monopoly of the station bookstalls.

St. Clement Danes Church, at the east end of the Strand, is said to have been so called because the Danes who remained after Alfred's final victory were made to live in this quarter. The church is of extreme antiquity. That which was taken down in 1680 was certainly not the earliest. In its churchyard lie the remains of King Harold. The new church was built by Edward Pierce, under the superintendence of Wren. The present tower and steeple were added by Gibbs. St. Clement's has long been famous for its bells, commented on in the children's game:

"Oranges and lemonsSay the bells of St. Clement's."

Oranges and lemons used to be distributed among the parish poor at certain seasons. The bells, ten in number, still peal as merrily as of old. In the gallery a brass plate with an inscription marks the spot where Dr. Johnson regularly sat in his attendance at service. The body of the church is filled with high old-fashioned pews, and the pulpit is a peculiarly rich bit of work attributed to Grinling Gibbons, though it does not altogether follow the usual type of his designs. Several monuments hang on the walls and pillars, but none of any general interest. In the church are buried Otway and Nathaniel Lee. The plate belonging to the church is very handsome and valuable, of silver, and some pieces date back to the time of Queen Elizabeth. The registers also commence at 1558, and contain several interesting entries. One of the earliest is the baptism of Robert Cecil, June 6, 1563, son of the High Treasurer, who was himself Prime Minister under Elizabeth and James I.

Essex Street recalls the fascinating and unhappy Essex, favourite of Queen Elizabeth. Essex House was built on the above-mentioned piece of ground called the Outer Temple which never belonged to the lawyers, but had been annexed by the Bishops of Exeter in the reign of the second Edward. This was then known as Exeter House. It was sacked by the populace in the same reign, and the unlucky prelate Walter Stapledon, who had taken the side of the King in his disputes with the Queen, was carried off and beheaded. The house was rebuilt, and continued to belong to the See until the reign of Henry VIII. But it seemed to have some malignant influence, for nearly all its successive owners suffered some unhappy fate. Lord Paget, who occupied it during Henry VIII.'s reign, narrowly escaped being beheaded. Thomas Howard, fourth son of the Duke of Norfolk, who succeeded, died in the Tower after many years of imprisonment. Dudley, Earl of Leicester, followed, and during his period of residence the house can claim association with the name of Spenser, who was a frequent visitor. Leicester escaped the malevolent influence of the house, which he left to his son-in-law, Robert Devereux, Earl of Essex. During the Earl's occupancy the mansion went through some stormy scenes. It was here that he assembled his fellow-conspirators which he left to his step-son, Robert Devereux, to arouse the people to aid him to obtain possession of the Queen's person, but he found his popularity unequal to the demand. The people turned against him, and he was driven back to his own house, which he barricaded. But his resistance was useless. Artillery was employed against him, and a gun mounted on the tower of St. Clement's Church. He was forced to surrender, and being found guilty of high treason, was executed. After the Restoration the house was let in tenements. It was pulled down about the end of the seventeenth century, but the Watergate at the end of the street is said to have been a part of it. The street was built in 1862. Dr. Johnson established here a small club known as the Essex Head Club.

The Essex Street Chapel, which was the headquarters of the Unitarians in London, was built upon part of the site of the house; Smith says it was part of the original building. The Cottonian Library was kept here from 1712 to 1730. A lecture-hall now stands on the site of the chapel. The Ethical Society give lectures here on Sunday evenings.

With Temple Bar the City of London, or, rather, the Liberties thereof, begin, and it is here that on great state occasions the Lord Mayor meets his Sovereign and hands to him the keys of the City. The first building on this spot was a timber house, but the exact date of its erection cannot be ascertained. It was probably put up for the decoration of a pageant, and, being found useful, was kept up. The gate has been often taken to have been part of the defences of the City, which it certainly was not, being protected or strengthened with neither moat nor drawbridge, nor being strong enough for the mounting of cannon. The Bar, a simple arrangement of chain and rails, is mentioned as early as 1301, but it cannot be ascertained that there was any building upon it. In 1502 the custody of the Bar, together with that of Newgate and Ludgate, is assigned to Alderman Fabian and others.

In 1533 it would seem that a gate was standing here, because for the reception of Anne Boleyn Temple Bar was newly painted and repaired, "whereon stood divers singing men and children." Again in 1547, for the coronation of Edward VI., the Bar was painted and fashioned with battlements. In 1554 the "new gates" of Temple Bar were assigned to the custody of the City. Aggas's map shows the Bar as a covered gate. The gateway was very cumbersome, blocking up an already narrow street.

Among other ceremonies it witnessed the progresses of Queen Elizabeth and Queen Anne respectively, to return thanks in St. Paul's Cathedral, the one for deliverance from the Armada, and the other in gratitude for Marlborough's victories. Inigo Jones, when he was engaged upon the Restoration of St. Paul's, was invited to furnish a design for a new arch. He complied, but his design was never carried out. It was engraved in 1727.

The Great Fire was checked before it reached Temple Bar. In 1670, however, the old gate was removed and its successor built by Wren. The familiar gate, still (1902) remembered by everybody who has reached manhood, was removed in the year 1878, and a monument with the City Dragon, colloquially known as the Griffin, was put up on the site of the Bar. The stones of the ancient building were preserved, and have been rebuilt in the park of Sir H. Meux at Cheshunt. One of the decorations of the later gateway consisted of iron spikes on which the heads of traitors were displayed, notably those of the men incriminated in the rebellions of the eighteenth century. When a high wind arose, these heads were sometimes blown down into the street below, a sight better to be imagined than described. From this circumstance Temple Bar was sometimes called the Golgotha of London.

Here we turn westward, and resume our perambulation in the part lying along the northern side of the Strand, which has not yet been described.

The parish of St. Clement Danes has changed very greatly since ancient times, when a large part of it, stretching from Lincoln's Inn Fields to the Strand, was known as Fickett's Field, and was the jousting-place of the Templars. This portion became gradually covered with houses and courts, which were at first fashionable dwelling-places, and were associated with noble names. These degenerated until, at the beginning of the present century, a vast rookery of noisome tenements, inhabited by the poorest and most wretched people, covered the greater part of the parish to the north of the Strand. The erection of the new Law Courts, 1868, entirely swept away numbers of these tenements, and opened out the parish to the north of the church. The change thus effected paved the way for further reformation, and though the streets about the site of Clare Market are poor and squalid, they show a beginning of better things, and no longer own such an evil reputation as they did.

Further north, beyond King's College Hospital, is Portugal Street, called by Strype "Playhouse Street." In the times of the later Stuarts it was a very fashionable locality. It is said that women first performed on the stage in public at the King's Theatre, in this street. The players were often patronized by Pepys. In 1717 the first English opera was performed here, and in 1727 the "Beggar's Opera" was produced with unprecedented success; but in 1835 the theatre in Portugal Street was taken down to make room for the enlargement of the museum belonging to the College of Surgeons.

Portsmouth Street contains a quaint, low, red-tiled house purporting to be the Old Curiosity Shop of Dickens' novel. The Black Jack Tavern, of some notoriety, stood here. It was the resort of the actors and dramatists of the adjacent theatre, and was the scene of a famous escape of Jack Sheppard from the Bow Street officers. It is said to have been a meeting-place of the Cato Street conspirators.

Shear or Shire Lane formerly ran from the east end of Carey Street to the Strand, and formed the parish boundary. This was a narrow, dirty lane of the vilest reputation before its demolition, but it had known better days. A very famous tavern stood in the lane, first called the Cat and Fiddle, later the Trumpet, and still later the Duke of York's. The well-known Kitcat Club met here originally. This was a society of thirty-nine gentlemen or noblemen zealously attached to the Protestant succession in the House of Hanover, and originated about 1700. Addison and Steele, Congreve, Vanbrugh, and others of celebrity, besides the Dukes of Somerset, Devonshire, Marlborough, Newcastle, etc., and many others, titled and untitled, were of the society. The bookseller Tonson was the secretary, and he had his own and all their portraits painted by Sir Godfrey Kneller, who was also a member of the club. Addison dated many of his famous essays from this address. The lane was known in the reign of the first James as Rogues' Lane.

The south side of Lincoln's Inn Fields only is within our boundaries, but the square is worth seeing. It is the largest in London, and was partly designed by Inigo Jones, who built the west side, called the Arch Row; the east side was bounded by the garden wall of Lincoln's Inn; on the north was Holborn Row; the south side was Portugal Row. The history of Lincoln's Inn Fields is a curious combination of rascality and of aristocracy. The rascals infested the fields, which were filled with wrestlers, rogues and cheats, pick-pockets, cripples and footpads; the aristocrats occupied the stately houses on the west side. Among the residents here were Lord Somers, the Duke of Newcastle, Lord Kenyon, Lord Erskine, and Spencer Percival. In the fields Babington and his accomplices were executed, some of them on the 20th, and some on the 21st, of September, 1586. Here also on July 21, 1683, William, Lord Russell was beheaded.

East of Drury Lane there lies a curious district mainly made up of lanes now rapidly disappearing, such as Clare Market, Wild Street, and a network of narrow courts. In 1657 Howell speaks of the Earl of Clare as living "in a princely manner" in this neighbourhood. It was in Clare Market that Orator

Henley had his chapel. The market was one chiefly for meat, and the shops and sheds were mainly occupied by butchers. Dr. Radcliffe frequented a tavern in this place, and Mrs. Bracegirdle, the actress, used to visit the market in order to assist the poor basket-women. The place is now almost gone. There was a notorious burial-ground, closed at last after its enormities had been exposed over and over again. King's College Hospital is built upon a part of the slums. Clement's Inn will be swept away by the Strand improvements. New Inn is still standing; Danes' Inn is a modern court with offices and residential chambers. Wych Street itself has still some of the old houses left. In Newcastle Street was Lyons' Inn, cleared away to make room for a theatre.

Drury Lane derives its name from the family mansion of the Druries which stood on the site. The brave Lord Craven bought this house and rebuilt it. It is stated that he married privately the Queen of Bohemia, daughter of James I. Timbs says that she occupied the house adjoining Craven House, which was connected with it by a subterranean passage. Craven Buildings were built in 1723 upon the site of the house; Hayman, the artist, and Mrs. Bracegirdle, the actress, both had rooms in these buildings. The Olympic Theatre is also partly on the site of Craven House.

Drury Lane was once a fashionable quarter, but lost that reputation before many of its contemporaries, and since the time of the third William has borne a more or less vile character. Nell Gwynne was born in Coal Yard, which opens off on the east side.

The Drury Lane Theatre has many interesting associations. It was built by Killigrew in 1663, and was called the King's House, under which title Pepys recalls many visits to it. In 1671 it was burnt down. It was rebuilt by Sir Christopher Wren, and opened 1674. Among the list of patentees we have the names of Rich, Steele, Doggett, Wilks, Cibber, Booth, and also Garrick, who began here his Shakespearian revivals. Sheridan succeeded Garrick as part proprietor, and in 1788 John Kemble became manager. The old theatre was demolished in 1791, and a new one opened three years after. This was also burned down in 1809, and the present theatre opened three years later. J. T. Smith takes the origin of the theatre still further back, saying that even from the time of Shakespeare there had been a theatre here, which had been a cockpit. The site of the cockpit, however, is on the other side of Drury Lane, where Pit Place now is.

North of the theatre was a disused burial-ground, later asphalted and turned into a public playground. It was less than a quarter of an acre in extent. It is now built over by workmen's dwellings of the usual kind. It was an additional burial-ground to St. Mary's le Strand, and is mentioned by Dickens in "Bleak House."

Crown Court recalls the Crown Tavern where *Punch* was first projected. The south end of Drury Lane, running into Wych Street, is now completely altered. New Inn and Booksellers' Row, otherwise Holywell Street, are wiped off the map, and the semicircular arm of the great new street connecting Holborn and the Strand will come out near St. Clement's Church. The name Holywell referred to a holy well which stood on the spot. There were, apparently, several of these wells in the vicinity; one was on the site of the Law Courts (*Times*, May 1, 1874). The street was a survival of old London, with its houses picturesquely old, with pointed gables, and it is a cause for regret that it had to go down in the march of modern improvements (see *frontispiece*).

Butcher Row ran round the north side of the church. It was so named from a flesh-market established here by Edward I. Numerous small courts opened off in the north side. Among these were Hemlock, Swan, Chair, Crown and Star Courts. The Row and its vicinity had for many years a notoriously bad reputation. One of the courts off Little Shear Alley was Boswell Court, not, as some have imagined, called after Johnson's biographer. This court was at one time a very fashionable place of residence; Lady Raleigh, the widow of Sir Walter, lived here for three years.

In Butcher Row the houses were picturesque, of timber and plaster. In one of them the great de Rosny, afterwards Duc de Sully, lodged for one night when he came to England as the French Ambassador.

Turning westward, we see what is left of Newcastle Street, which was named after John Holles, Duke of Newcastle, who owned the ground (1711). The work of demolition is going on as far as Catherine Street, where the Gaiety theatre still stands, though not for long, for the second great scimitar sweep of the new street will join the Strand here.

The parish of St. Paul's lies like a leaf on the parish of St. Martin's-in-the-Fields, by which it is wholly surrounded. Its southern boundary runs most erratically, zigzagging in and out across the streets which connect Maiden Lane and Henrietta Street with the Strand. The eastern line keeps on the east side of Bow and Brydges Street. The north passes along the north side of Hart Street, and the west cuts across the east ends of Garrick and New Streets, keeping to the east of Bedfordbury.

The name Covent is a corruption of Convent, and is taken from the convent garden of the Abbey of Westminster, which was formerly on this site. It was written Covent, as taken from the French *couvent* more immediately than the Latin *conventus*.

At the dissolution of the monasteries, Westminster Convent Garden became Crown property. In the first year of his reign Edward VI. granted it to the Duke of Somerset. On the fall of that nobleman it reverted to the Crown, and in 1552 was granted to the Earl of Bedford with "seven acres, called Long Acre." The Earl of Bedford built a town-house on his newly acquired property, and devoted himself to the improvement of the neighbourhood.

Though the parish is so small, it is full of interesting associations, chiefly of the last two centuries. Wits, actors, literary men, and artists, frequented its taverns and swarmed in its precincts. The contrast between its earlier days, when it was a quiet retreat where the monks slowly paced beneath the sheltering trees, and its later vicissitudes, when the eighteenth-century roisterers and gamesters made merry within its taverns, could hardly be more striking.

The great square called the Market was laid out by the Earl of Bedford in 1631; the Piazza ran along the north and east sides; the church and churchyard formed the west side; on the south was the wall of Bedford House, and by a small grove of trees in the middle stood a sundial. The place gradually grew as a market. In 1710 there were only a few sheds; in 1748 the sheds had become tenements, with upper rooms inhabited by bakers, cooks and retailers of gin.

The square itself is redolent of memories. When first built it was one of the most fashionable parts of London, and the names of the occupiers were all titled or distinguished. We read among them those of the Bishop of Durham, Duke of Richmond, Earl of Oxford, Marquis of Winchester, Sir Godfrey Kneller, and the Earl of Sussex. The arcade, or Piazza, as it was called, was a fashionable lounging-place, and many foundling children were called Piazza in its honour. One of the scenes in Otway's "Soldier of Fortune" is laid here, and also one in Wycherley's "Country Wife." Sir Peter Lely had a house in the square, and this house was successively occupied by Sir Godfrey Kneller and Sir James Thornhill (Timbs). Coffee-houses and taverns abounded in and about the square. Of these the most famous were Will's, Button's and Tom's, well known by the references to them in contemporary literature. The first of these in point of time was "Will's," which stood at the north corner of Russell and Bow Streets (see p. 106).

The Bedford Coffee-house under the Piazza succeeded Button's, or, rather, came into vogue afterwards when Garrick, Quin, Foote and others used it. The house stood at the north-east corner. It is described as a place of resort for critics. "Everyone you meet is a polite scholar and critic ... the merit of every production of the press is weighed and determined." Apparently a place where the conversation was a continual attempt at smartness; it must have been most fatiguing. The weak point, indeed, of this public life was the demand it created for conversational display. The greater part of

Johnson's pithy sayings were delivered in such a mixed company, and were prepared in sonorous English to suit the company.

An article in the *London Mercury*, January 13, 1721, states that there were twenty-two gaming-houses in the parish. Besides all these attractions, there was Covent Garden theatre opened in 1733 by Rich, though the first patent had been granted to Sir William Davenant. In 1746 Garrick joined Rich, but at the end of the season left him for Drury Lane, taking with him all the best actors. In 1803 Kemble became proprietor and stage-manager, but five years later the theatre was completely burnt. It was rebuilt under the directions of R. Smirke, and when re-opened was the scene of a singularly pertinacious revolt. The prices had been raised in consequence of the improved accommodation, and the people in the pit banded themselves together under the name of "Old Prices," and made such an intolerable uproar that the piece could not proceed. Smith says "the town seemed to have lost its senses." For weeks people wore O.P. hats and O.P. handkerchiefs, and interrupted every attempt to carry the play through. In the end a compromise was made. In 1840 Charles Kemble left the theatre, and the building was leased to C. Mathews, Madame Vestris and Macready. In 1847 it was opened as an Italian Opera-House after being almost rebuilt. It was again destroyed by fire in 1856, but the façade was saved with its bas-reliefs and statues by Flaxman and Rossi. These were placed on the present building designed by Barry, which was opened two years later.

The Church of St. Paul, Covent Garden, was built by Inigo Jones in 1633 at the expense of the Earl of Bedford; consecrated by Bishop Juxon in 1638; destroyed by fire in 1795; rebuilt by John Hardwick in the place of the original building. And the story goes that when the architect heard the commission, "to build a church not much bigger than a barn," he replied it should be the handsomest barn in England.

Buried here are Robert Carr, Earl of Somerset; Sir Henry Herbert and Samuel Butler, author of "Hudibras," died 1680; Sir Peter Lely, died 1680, whose monument was destroyed in the fire; Edward Kynaston, actor; Wycherley, the dramatist; Grinling Gibbons, died 1721, sculptor in wood; Susannah Centlivre; Dr. Arne, musician, died 1778; Charles Macklin, comedian, died 1797 at the age of 107; John Wolcott, *alias* Peter Pindar, died 1819. The registers begin at 1615, and among the baptismal entries are the names of Lady Mary Wortley Montagu, May 26, 1689, and Turner, the painter, May 14, 1775.

The church is visible from the street on the east and the market on the west, but accessible only by a covered entry under the houses on the north and south. In Hogarth's picture of "Morning" we get a glimpse of the old church before its destruction, with clock-dial, and tiled roof, not so very dissimilar from what it is at present.

The election of members for Westminster formerly took place on a hustings before the church, when there were scenes of wild riot. The most memorable of these elections was that of Fox and Sir Cecil Wray in 1784.

Bow Street, Covent Garden, was built in 1637, and named after its shape, that of a bent bow. It is remarkable for the number of well-known persons who have lived in it. It was one of the most fashionable streets in the Metropolis, and Dryden wrote in the epilogue to one of his plays:

"I've had to-day a dozen billet-douxFrom fops and wits and cits and Bow Street beaux;"

on which Sir Walter Scott remarked a billet-doux from Bow Street would now be more alarming than flattering. The police officer began his reign here in 1749.

Henry Fielding, who was in authority in 1753, did much to suppress the unbridled license and open highway robbery of the Metropolis.

Will's Coffee-house was at No. 1, on the west side, the corner of Russell Street. The principal room was on the first floor. Dryden made the house the chief place of resort for the poets and wits of the time. After his death Addison took the company across the street to Button's. Ned Ward's notes on Will's are not respectful.

"From thence we adjourned to the Wits' Coffee-house.... Accordingly, upstairs we went, and found much company, but little talk.... We shuffled through this moving crowd of philosophical mutes to the other end of the room, where three or four wits of the upper class were rendezvous'd at a table, and were disturbing the ashes of the old poets by perverting their sense.... At another table were seated a parcel of young, raw, second-rate beaus and wits, who were conceited if they had but the honour to dip a finger and thumb into Mr. Dryden's snuff-box" (Cunningham, p. 555.).

Defoe, on the other hand, is more complimentary:—

"Now view the beaus at Will's, the men of wit,
By nature nice, and for discerning fit,
The finished fops, the men of wig and muff.
Knights of the famous oyster-barrel snuff."

At Button's there was a carved lion's head, of which the mouth was a letter-box for contributions to the *Guardian* and *Tatler*. This was set up by

Addison in 1713, and attracted much attention. It was removed in 1731 to the Shakespeare Tavern, and later came into the possession of the Duke of Bedford. Tom's was the last of the three famous houses. It was started by a waiter from Will's, and managed to hold its own. It was on the north side of the street, nearly opposite Button's.

The literary associations of the street are innumerable. Wycherley lodged here, and after an illness was visited by Charles II., who gave him £500 for a trip to France. The well-known Cock Tavern was just opposite his rooms, and when Wycherley had married the Countess of Drogheda he used to sit in the tavern with the windows open so that his jealous wife could see there were no women in his company. This tavern was the resort of the rakes and mohocks that for a while made the neighbourhood a terror to decent people. Henry Fielding wrote "Tom Jones" while living in this street. Grinling Gibbons died here. Edmund Waller, the poet, lived here during the Commonwealth, and Robert Harley, Earl of Oxford, was born here in 1661. Radcliffe, the Court physician, was a resident in the beginning of the eighteenth century.

The streets opening out of the square can boast many interesting associations.

Henrietta Street was named after Charles I.'s Queen. Samuel Cooper, miniature-painter, lived here. The Castle Tavern, where Sheridan fought with Mathews on account of Miss Linley, was in this street.

Maiden Lane can claim several illustrious names. It was the birthplace of Turner; Andrew Marvell and Voltaire both lodged here.

Long Acre was originally an open field called the Elms, and later known as Seven Acres, from a grant of land made to the Duke of Bedford. A curious house-to-house survey of 1650 is preserved in the Augmentation Office. From this it would appear that the street at that date was full of small shops, grocers, chandlers, etc., with here and there a big house occupied by some titled person. Ever since the first introduction of coaches Long Acre has been particularly favoured by coachbuilders, and at the present time it is lined by carriage-works. Long Acre was the scene of many convivial gatherings in the Hanoverian times. It can claim the first "mug-house," an institution which speedily became popular. Oliver Cromwell lived on the south side of Long Acre, and Dryden and Butler in Rose Street, a dirty little alley half destroyed by the building of Garrick Street. Here Dryden was set upon by three hired bullies at the command of Lord Rochester, who was insulted by some satirical lines which he attributed to the poet.

Garrick Street was built about 1864, and the club of the same name was founded for the patronage of dramatic art.

St. Martin's Lane is one of the oldest thoroughfares in the parish. It was built about 1613, and was then known as West Church Lane. It ran right through to the front of Northumberland House, and prints are still extant showing the church peeping over the line of houses on the western side.

St. Martin's Lane claims many celebrated names, and was a favourite resort for artists. The house in which Inigo Jones lived is still pointed out—No. 31 on the east side. Almost exactly opposite this is the Public Library, built at the same time as the Municipal Buildings; it contains a fine reference collection (see also p. 21.) The lane abounds with memories of the past. In St. Peter's Court Roubiliac established a studio, afterwards a drawing academy, which numbered Hayman, Cipriani, Ramsay, Cosway, Nollekens, Reynolds and Hogarth among its members; this was the predecessor of the Royal Academy. This court was two or three doors above the Free Library, and was eventually closed up at the west end by the Garrick Theatre. No. 114 is traditionally on the site of the mansion of the Earls of Salisbury, in which, also traditionally, the Seven Bishops were confined before being committed to the Tower. The names of Chippendale, Nathaniel Hone and Fuseli are associated with the lane, also Sir Joshua Reynolds and Sir James Thornhill.

Old Slaughter's Coffee-house alone is enough to redeem any street from oblivion. This was established in 1692, and stood on the spot where Cranbourne Street now crosses the end of St. Martin's Lane. It was a favourite resort of all the painters and sculptors of the time, not to mention the wits and beaux. Hogarth was a constant visitor, his house in Leicester Square being conveniently near. Roubiliac, Gainsborough, and also Wilkie, came to enjoy society at Old Slaughter's, and Pope and Dryden are known to have visited it. The first chess club in London was established here in 1747.

And now we have strolled around the chosen area, making Trafalgar Square the centre, and returning to and fro in two great loops eastward and westward, resembling a true lovers' knot. We have been in the company of King and courtier, rebel and wit. We have consorted with the gay fops of the eighteenth century in their club and coffee house life, and we have seen the haunts of men whose names are household words wherever the English tongue is spoken.

It has been chiefly seventeenth and eighteenth century life that has enchained us as we read the pages of the past, and in its richness and variety at least the eighteenth century would be difficult to rival. Prosaic London, with her borough councils, her Strand improvements, and her immense utilitarian flats, still retains the glamour of her bygone days, and if her present buildings are without much attraction, they are glorified by the halo of their association with their fascinating predecessors.

Milton Keynes UK
Ingram Content Group UK Ltd.
UKHW030913151124
451262UK00006B/764